Building
Positive
Thinking
Habits

Building Positive Thinking Habits

Increasing Self-Confidence & Resilience in Young People through CBT

TINA RAE

HINTON HOUSE Emotional Literacy Resources

HINTONHOUSE

First published in 2016 by
Hinton House Publishers Ltd, Newman House, 4 High Street, Buckingham, MK18 1NT, UK
T +44 (0)1280 822557 F +44 (0)1280 822338 E info@hintonpublishers.com
www.hintonpublishers.com

© 2016 Tina Rae

Reprinted 2017, 2020

British Library Cataloguing in Publication Data
A CIP catalogue record for this book is available from the British Library.

ISBN 978 1 906531 76 8
Printed and bound in the United Kingdom

Contents

Acknowledgements   vii
About the Author   vii

Introduction   1
   Why Positive Psychology?   2
   The Importance of Positive Emotions   3
   Teaching Effective Thinking – the Positive Impact   5
   The Tools to Support Well-Being 1 – Cognitive Behavioural
      Therapy (CBT)   6
   The Tools to Support Well-Being 2 – Using Motivational
      Interviewing (MI) to Promote Positive Behavioural Change   9
   Objectives of the Programme   11
   About the Programme   12
   The Structure of the Sessions   13

The Sessions
1 Thinking about Thinking   15
2 NATs & PATs   27
3 Doing Yourself Down   35
4 Self-Image Issues   43
5 What Influences Us?   51
6 Core Beliefs & Making the Connections   61
7 Beat the Blues   71
8 The Change Cycle   79
9 How to See Failure   91
10 Test Your Thinking   99
11 My Wants & SMART Targets   107
12 Building Positive Thinking Habits   117
13 Chillax   125
14 Positive Selfie   133
15 Reflect, Evaluate & Persist!   145

Appendices

Appendix 1 Information for Parents and Carers

What is Cognitive Behavioural Therapy (CBT)?   154

Consent Form for the Programme   155

Suggestions for Parents, Carers & Teachers on

Managing Anxiety   156

Mental Health Fact Sheet   158

Appendix 2 References & Bibliography

CBT with Children & Young People: Useful References   160

Outcome Literature   162

Assessment References   163

Acknowledgements

My thanks go to Sarah Miles at Hinton House Publishers.

About the Author

Dr Tina Rae has more thirty years' experience working with children, adults and families in both clinical and educational contexts within local authorities and specialist educational services. She currently works as a consultant educational and child psychologist in a range of SEBD/SEMH and mainstream contexts and for Compass Fostering as a consultant psychologist supporting foster carers, social workers and looked-after children. She is an academic and professional tutor for the Doctorate in Educational and Child Psychology at the University of East London. She is a registered member of the Health and Care Professions Council, a full member of the British Psychological Society, and a member of the editorial board for the SEBDA journal *Emotional and Behavioural Difficulties* and for the *International Journal of Nurture in Education*. Tina is also a member of the SEBDA council and executive, a member of ENSEC (European Network for Social and Emotional Competence) and, until recently, a trustee of the Nurture Group Network (NGN).

Tina has published more than 75 titles on topics including well-being, attachment, emotional literacy, behavioural problems, anger and stress management, critical incidents, cognitive behavioural therapy, motivational interviewing, solution-focused brief therapy, loss and bereavement in young people, youth offending and social skills development.

Her current research is into staff well-being and resilience, including peer group supervision systems.

Tina is a regular speaker at both national and international conferences and events, and also provides training courses and supervision for school-based staff in both special and mainstream contexts and educational psychology services across the UK and internationally.

tinarae@hotmail.co.uk
t.m.rae@uel.ac.uk

Introduction

This resource aims to support young people in the development of effective thinking which, in turn, maintains overall well-being and mental health. According to a 2013 survey of 844 education staff by the Association of Teachers and Lecturers (ATL), the number of children and young people in school with behavioural, emotional or mental health problems is rising in the UK. This increase is coupled with apparently worsening student behaviour in schools and colleges; according to the OECD's 'Teaching and Learning International Survey' (June 2014), more than a fifth of teachers in the United Kingdom regularly struggle to control rowdy lessons and were more likely to be verbally abused by pupils than in almost any other country. Dr Mary Bousted, general secretary of the ATL, believes the solution to this problem is to properly equip teachers with the skills to manage students with behavioural and mental health problems:

> *Regrettably teachers and support staff are suffering the backlash from deteriorating standards of behaviour. They are frequently on the receiving end of children's frustration and unhappiness, and have to deal with the fall-out from parents failing to set boundaries and family breakdowns. And the huge funding cuts to local services mean that schools often have to deal with children's problems without any help ... Schools must give their staff good and regular training so that they know how to work with students with behavioural or mental health problems and have confidence in handling pupils with challenging behaviour.(2013)*

The ATL survey also highlighted a deficit in training to support students with mental health problems – only a fifth (21 per cent) of teachers get regular training, which they rate as good or adequate, and nearly 39 per cent said they did not get any relevant training in their initial teacher training. Considering that teachers are now more likely to be in contact with children experiencing mental health problems than the primary health care, mental health services and social services combined (Ford, 2014), it is of the utmost importance that teachers receive appropriate training to ensure that they are able not only to identify mental health issues, but also to engage in preventative work. This resource will hopefully provide a means of engaging therapeutically with young people and support staff in developing their knowledge of key tools and strategies that promote positive thinking and self-concepts in children and young people.

Although access to therapy is not seen as the 'norm' in the majority of educational contexts, with the increase of mental health difficulties amongst our children and young people and the complex pressures that they face growing up, knowledge of therapeutic approaches is becoming essential for ALL who work in the educational sector. Many staff feel relatively skilled in terms of providing academic and social support to young people, but there remains a real feeling and evident concern that they do not have the knowledge base or level of skills required to specifically support those with more complex and emerging mental health difficulties. Yet in past trials teachers who were taught the same techniques and approaches used by psychologists when intervening with anxious children were shown to have as many, if not more, positive results than psychologists (Barrett & Turner, 2001).

The suggestion here is not to promote the notion of staff seeking to become or take on the role of 'the therapist', but to recognise that they would be more effective in terms of identifying and preventing the escalation of mental health difficulties if they were more skilled and knowledgeable in utilising therapeutic skills and approaches.

Positive psychology has been described as a scientific study of subjective well-being. This is the technical term for what we would call 'happiness' and the factors that enable us as individuals in order to grow and develop and sustain ourselves in a positive manner. Key to the approach is the focus on what actually works for us as individuals, as opposed to the continual analysing of what has gone wrong or what we are not good at. This is particularly important given the current prevalence of mental health issues amongst our young people. The fact that approximately 1 in 10 young people suffer from a diagnosable mental health disorder, which would amount to three students in every class, is reason enough why the school-based staff should focus on the development of key skills to promote resilience and happiness. Mental health should clearly be linked to, or described as, an increase in the general degree of happiness, vitality, sense of self-worth and achievement alongside an individual's concern and empathy for others. Within a school-based context this would suggest that any curriculum should actively prevent unhappiness, for example bullying, violence and conflict, whilst encouraging learners and those supporting them in schools to achieve their goals, to feel love, to feel joyful, to be energetic and to care about others (Weare, 2000).

Why Positive Psychology?

In recent years there have been a plethora of initiatives in terms of supporting the emotional well-being and social and emotional skills development of young people. This includes the development of healthy schools policies that include mental, social and emotional health: in other words policies that actively prevent bullying, violence and conflict. In schools there has also been a focus through the Personal, Social & Health Education (PSHE) and Social & Emotional Aspects of Learning (SEAL) curriculum on including and developing personal and emotional literacy skills amongst staff and young people alike. The creation of supportive environments where all individuals actively and openly care for each other has also been promoted as best practice.

The goal of positive psychology is basically to enhance human strengths such as optimism, courage, honesty, self-understanding and interpersonal skills. This is the opposite of what Dr Martin Seligman (2011) calls 'focusing on the broken things and on repairing the damage of past traumas'. Positive psychology provides a means of helping the individual to use inner resources as a buffer against setbacks and adversity in life whenever these crop up. Developing such skills helps to prevent individuals from becoming depressed. As Seligman states, 'it's not about how to heal; it's about to have a great life'.

Seligman and his associates developed an intervention designed to instil a sense of optimism, which they defined as a positive way of construing the failures and setbacks that normally occur in life. This is similar to approaches utilised in cognitive behavioural therapy, in which participants are encouraged to construe failures in a more positive light. For example, if you consider that failures are stable and pervasive, then they will last forever and subsequently undermine everything that you try to do – this will ultimately lead to depression. However, if we can train young people and ourselves to view such setbacks and difficulties as temporary or affecting only a small part of our lives, then the depression can be averted.

In a recent project involving university students, psychologists screened the students using a questionnaire that measured their optimism and resilience. The students who scored the lowest for optimism were then randomly assigned to either low intervention or to a workshop designed to develop skills in boosting their own optimism. Key amongst these workshop-taught skills was the CBT approach known as 'Disputing'. Students were taught to recognise their negative automatic thoughts about themselves and to then argue against these thoughts as if they were disputing them as an external critic. Of the 126 subjects who took part, 119 controls were then followed up for between eight and ten years. It was particularly pleasing that during young adulthood those who had participated in the positive psychology programme when they were in college were half as likely to have had episodes of moderate unipolar depression (13 per cent) as with the control subjects (27 per cent). Similarly, the subjects who had taken part in the workshops had half the rate of generalised anxiety disorders compared with the controls.

The Importance of Positive Emotions

Central to any positive psychology approach in schools, therefore, is a focus upon ensuring that young people have optimum opportunities to experience positive emotions. This will ensure their ability to attend to lessons, increase working memory and verbal fluency, and also ensure an increased openness to information. Seligman highlights three essential areas that are key to the experience of happiness and well-being:

- Hope & optimism
- Flow
- Happy memories

All three of these can be seen to improve learning in the classroom.

Hope & Optimism

Building hope and optimism is clearly a key aspect of education. Young people will generally learn if they feel hopeful about their own skills and their future lives, and it is optimism which ensures that both young people and adults can develop resiliency skills; bouncing back from adversity and remaining in control of their own emotions and behaviours. Resiliency is something that develops through positive relationships and it is vital, according to positive psychologists, that young people have the opportunity to develop these traits while living what has been termed a 'connected childhood'. This involves having at least one adult who believes totally in their worth and abilities and who also has the capacity and commitment to redirect the young person towards being productive, successful and happy.

Flow

Key to promoting and maintaining this optimism is the concept of flow. This is defined as a sense of deep engagement in an activity during which time passes extremely quickly and the individual is able to work at full capacity. Nothing distracts them as they learn and make progress towards their ultimate goals. The aftermath to this state is truly invigorating as the individual will feel happy and relaxed with a sense of achievement. This is something that we should strive for with any young person. However, translating this kind of absorption into more formal learning settings can be a challenge, in that it is easier to achieve flow in activities which are self-selected and intrinsically enjoyable. What is essential is that the challenge is relevant to the task. If it is too great, the young person will feel anxious or frustrated, whereas when it is appropriate (in other words, there is a good balance between the skills and the demands of the challenge) then the young person will succeed and begin to achieve this state of flow.

Happy Memories

Happy memories are, as Seligman stated, 'extremely important for ensuring happiness and well-being; the way that we feel about the past and our experiences can clearly impact both positively and negatively on how we feel and function at the present time.' Students in classrooms who only remember how badly they did last time are likely to underperform in the present – this is basic common sense. What teachers need to do is to encourage students to pay attention to what they did well and what they got right, particularly when struggling with new challenges.

Focusing on the Positive

The key strategy taught in any positive psychology intervention is that of reframing. It is extremely important to ensure that young people are able to build and use happy memories, whilst also reframing any negative automatic thoughts that they might experience. It is also vital to reflect upon the kinds of stories that we tell ourselves and why things go wrong for us. It is generally a human trait, and quite normal for us, to view things in a negative manner. For example, 'That person gave me a dirty look so therefore they don't like me', as opposed to, 'That person looks a bit upset, I wonder if I can help them?' We frequently tell ourselves negative stories and use more pessimistic explanations; unfortunately these pessimistic explanations tend to undermine our ability to keep going when things go wrong for us. Young people need to have this constantly monitored and to learn to reflect upon the way in which their thinking is working. Part of any curriculum in this area should focus upon encouraging young people to tell themselves positive stories on a regular, possibly daily, basis. Also they need to be encouraged to build positive thought habits as these are both motivating and self-affirming.

Importance of Bravery

A further essential in the positive psychology approach is that of building bravery. It is vital to encourage young people to exercise courage and to push themselves beyond where their normal comfort zone would tell them to go. It is also clearly vital that everyone in the learning community is aware of the fact that failure is an inevitable consequence of this exercise of being brave. If we fail, then we know that we are working above and beyond our capacity and this can only be a positive thing. Failing at something is not the problem; the problem is when we get into a habit of giving up and retreating back into our comfort zones. If we fall into this pattern of behaviour we will never grow and develop; we will simply learn to fail or fail to learn, as Tal Ben-Shahar states.

A school that promotes positive psychology will ensure that all young people do not own their own failures in isolation. Failure is owned by teaching staff also, who should in turn ensure that they can problem-solve together with the young people. Praising, perseverance and the 'have a go' positive attitude is extremely important. Verbal and emotional recognition is much more valuable and important to young people than tangible rewards. As human beings we all want and thrive upon praise, the good opinion of others and the fact that we know that they basically care about us.

Teaching Effective Thinking – the Positive Impact

Positive psychology in essence enables schools to be inspiring, comforting, fun and exciting. When school-based staff make use of strategies to build such optimistic environments where positive emotions are promoted and young people's emotional resilience is fostered, then academic and social and emotional gains will be made for all involved.

Positive psychology has to be central to any approach in education in order to achieve such a goal. There is now a wealth of research to confirm that happy people are successful across all domains, including relationships, marriage, longevity, health, income and work performance. Our failure to promote this kind of well-being education would result in us failing to ensure the optimal functioning and development of young people in our care.

In simplistic terms I would argue that positive psychology can help us to learn and reinforce some of the following skills:

- To continually become aware of our positive experiences.
- To engage in things we enjoy and that give us a buzz.
- To be able to reframe our negative stories and experiences and continually tell ourselves what is positive about our lives.
- To foster flow and aim to remain in that state as much as possible.
- To recall happy memories when we are low.
- To move from our comfort zones to our stretched zones in order to further promote resilience, self-esteem and achievement.
- Not to be frightened to ask for help when we get stressed or find ourselves unable to cope.
- To have the courage to fail and learn from those failures.

The Tools to Support Well-Being 1 – Cognitive Behavioural Therapy (CBT)

A key set of tools can effectively be introduced to young people in schools in order to support the development of effective thinking and promote levels of self-confidence and resilience. This resource bank aims to utilise strategies from CBT in order to achieve such a goal. This evidence-based intervention can provide us with tools to encourage and maintain effective thinking which will, in turn, promote well-being overall.

Cognitive Behavioural Therapy is currently the 'therapy of choice' (Holmes, 2002, p.1). The delivery of CBT has become a central part of recent government initiatives (Department of Health, 2001, 2004, 2007), due to findings from random controlled trials indicating it is potentially seen as being more cost effective than medication (London School of Economics, 2007). This, alongside *Every Child Matters'* emphasis on children's health and well-being (DfES, 2004), has led educational psychologists in particular to question their position in the provision of psychotherapy for children's mental health issues (Farrell Report, 2006; Mackay, 2002) and whether CBT can be incorporated into educational psychology casework (Dunsmuir & Lyadurai, 2007; Greig, 2001 Greig & MacKay, 2005). Many therapists, counsellors, mentors and SENCOs are currently making use of CBT approaches in order to support positive change and emotional well-being in the young people they support. This kind of approach is a specific goal-orientated therapy, and it frequently results in positive change within a relatively short period of time. This is very unlike traditional psychotherapy, which can, for some individuals, take many years to produce any kind of positive result or outcome.

CBT reveals the role that thoughts play in relation to both our emotions and our behaviours. This approach provides individuals with a way of talking about themselves, their world and people who inhabit it, so that they are more able to understand how what they do effects both their thoughts and feelings, and vice versa.

This approach focuses on the role that thoughts play in regard to both emotions and behaviour, and advocates that change in thought processes can have a significant effect upon altering behaviours. Unlike many of the talking treatments that traditional therapists have used, CBT focuses upon the 'here and now', as well as ways to improve the individual's state of mind in the present time. This is innovative in the sense that there is no focus on the causes of distress or past symptoms as there evidently is with traditional psychotherapy.

Restructuring Thought Processes

Young people are frequently flooded with anxious and negative thoughts and doubts. These messages will often reinforce a state of inadequacy and/or low levels of *self-esteem*. The process of CBT helps to support young people in reconsidering these negative assumptions. It also allows them to *learn how* to change their self-perceptions in order to improve their mental and emotional state – this is the key aim of this kind of intervention. Changing negative thought patterns or opinions will ultimately help young people to become more able to control and change their behaviours, but this does take practice. This is why, as with anger management interventions, another key element of the approach is the requirement to learn, and to put into practice, the skills or strategies discussed in any session.

ABC

The CBT approach breaks any problem into smaller parts. This enables the young person to see how a problem comes to exist and how they themselves may be affected by the problem. This follows a process of A, B, C as follows:

- **A**, or the **activating event**, is often referred to as the 'trigger' – the thing that causes you to engage in the negative thinking.

- **B** represents these negative **beliefs**, which can include thoughts, rules and demands, and the meanings the individual attaches to both external and internal events.

- **C** is the **consequences**, or emotions, and the behaviours and physical sensations accompanying these different emotions. It is important to highlight and discuss with the group how the way that they think about a problem can affect how they feel physically and emotionally. It can also alter what they do about it. This is why the key aim for CBT is to break the negative, vicious cycle that some young people may find themselves in. For example, if you think that you will get your work wrong you feel angry, and then you don't give it a try in case it is wrong.

Core Beliefs

Core beliefs are the strong, enduring ideas that we may have about ourselves. This kind of belief system gives rise to rules, demands or assumptions, which in turn produce automatic thoughts. Core beliefs generally fall into three main categories: beliefs about yourself; beliefs about other people in the world; beliefs that are either positive or negative. What is important is to identify our core beliefs and to also consider why these may or may not be helpful. In this way we can begin to identify negative automatic thoughts (NATs).

What are NATs?

Negative core beliefs can cause us to engage in a number of faulty thinking strategies. Individuals will tend to focus on negative automatic thoughts (NATs). Some of these thoughts that young people may hold about themselves could include the following:

- I always look ugly.

- I don't understand this work.

- He thinks I'm stupid and an idiot.

- She gave me a nasty look.

- I'm just such a useless person.

- I can't do that and I'll never be able to do it like other people can.

When working with young people in identifying such faulty thinking, the main aim is to encourage them to break the negative cycle. These NATs can arise from a number of errors in our thinking, including the following six types of faulty thinking:

1. **Doing ourselves down** – only focusing on the negatives and seeing bad things about ourselves.

2. **Blowing things up or catastrophising** – making things worse than they really are.

3 Predicting failure – setting your mind ready to predict failure at all costs.

4 Over-emotional thoughts – this is when your emotions become extremely powerful and cloud your judgement.

5 Setting yourself up – setting yourself targets that are too high so that you know then you will fail.

6 Blaming yourself – thinking that everything that goes wrong is your own fault.

When working with young people, it is important to allow them time to consider the effects that these NATs can have prior to them beginning to implement some changes.

Behavioural Experiments

One of the most helpful interventions for developing new and more positive belief systems, and for challenging NATs, is to **test the evidence**. The group can engage in the following questioning process:

- What is the evidence for this thought?
- What is the evidence against this thought?
- What would my best friend say if they heard my thought?
- What would my teacher say if he heard my thought?
- What would my parents or carers say if they heard my thought?
- What would I say to my best friend if s/he had this same thought?
- Am I making mistakes? For example, 'blowing it up', forgetting my strengths or good points, self-blaming or predicting failure, or thinking that I can mind-read what others are thinking?

This kind of strategy is particularly useful in terms of reinforcing the need to gather accurate evidence. What we believe about ourselves is not always true. It is not how others always see us and these kinds of beliefs need to be challenged in this way. Using this sort of questioning process, and gathering evidence in the form of such a behavioural experiment, is a particularly positive strategy for beginning to identify and challenge unhelpful beliefs that young people may carry.

Further Strategies to Implement Change

Reframing is another useful tool for group members to learn and practise. Negative thoughts can be reframed into more positive, balanced and realistic ones. For example, 'I am just fat', could be reframed as 'I need to lose some weight and tone up a bit but my overall shape isn't that bad'; or 'I always get the maths work wrong', could be reframed as 'Some of these sums are difficult but I know I can do the basics – I just need to work hard and find help in order to improve my skills.'

Distraction is also a useful strategy by which to banish NATs. The group can be encouraged to control their thoughts by thinking of something else. For example:

- They can describe in detail what they see around them in order to feel calmer. They can attempt to name all of their favourite bands.

- They can use self-talk techniques and repeat a positive coping message until the NAT has gone.

- They can 'bin' the thoughts by writing them down and then screwing them up and putting them into the bin – symbolically eradicating these negative thoughts.

- Group members can also keep a positive diary in order to record positive automatic thoughts (PATs) that may occur during the day, and engage in realistic goal-setting, which involves practice.

Overall, what is important when young people are engaged in learning and developing these skills is for adults to encourage them to set appropriate targets. Young people need to be reminded that we do not move forwards unless we set realistic goals for ourselves. These should be broken down into small, achievable steps and the ultimate goal continually focused upon. Setting targets allows us to visualise where we want to be in the future and if we feel that we have nowhere to go, nor nothing to move towards, then ultimately we will not be able to affect the change necessary.

The Tools to Support Well-Being 2 – Using Motivational Interviewing Techniques (MI) to Promote Positive Behaviour Change

Motivational Interviewing (MI) is the second evidence-based intervention in our resource bank that can encourage and maintain effective thinking in pursuit of overall well-being. MI was originally developed by Miller & Rollnick (1991). It was defined as a person-centred, directive method for enhancing intrinsic motivation to change by exploring and resolving ambivalence. The central premise of the MI approach was that people are not always ready to change their behaviours. Consequently, there is no presumption or assumption that people actually want to change particular aspects of their behaviour. Behavioural change is then, in effect, reliant upon the individual's motivation.

Understanding Change

It is important, when working with young people, to emphasise the fact that people may not always be ready to change their patterns of behaviour. Motivational interviewing as an approach acknowledges this and the fact that many of us have good reasons for choosing to maintain our behaviours. For example, a young person who is 'badly' behaved may find it more fun and gain more attention from this behaviour than they would if they changed their behaviours and remained passive within the classroom setting.

Key to the approach is the focus on ambivalence. This is the uncomfortable feeling that we have when we are not sure whether or not we want to change. This is what young people need to be further attuned to if they are effectively to make changes for themselves that are not imposed by others within the learning or social context. It is also vital to emphasise the fact that change is not in itself a comfortable process.

Introduction

Exploring Ambivalence

Change is all about ambivalence. When we make a change, it is not just a matter of making a simple 'yes' or 'no' decision as there are always pros and cons to change. Sometimes the pros outweigh the cons and we can begin to move forward in the right direction. Sometimes the cons seem to outweigh the pros and then we can get stuck or relapse. Ambivalence is the bit in the middle that is a normal part of change and not a particularly comfortable place to be. Young people can be introduced to this concept when considering a change that other people might want to make on their behalf. For example, a form tutor might want the student to participate more fully in PSHE sessions and not simply sit at the back of the class giggling and making fun of everything that is said by other members of the peer group.

They can be asked to record a list of negatives ('I don't want to change this behaviour because ...'), and then a list of positives ('This is a good idea because ...'). Prior to making this list they may wish to rate themselves on a scale of 0–10. What do they think about this change? Do they agree that they need to make this change? Where would they place themselves on a scale of 0–10, where 0 is strongly opposed to the change and 10 is totally willing to accept it? After recording the negatives and positives, the pros and cons of making a particular change, they can then re-rate themselves. The aim is to reinforce the fact that once we start to analyse the problem and work out why we may need to change we can move forward from this uncomfortable position of ambivalence due to the fact that our thinking has shifted more in the direction of where we need to be.

The Stages of Change

Exploring the potential benefits of change is a key element of MI and is supported by increasing and understanding appreciation of the stages of change. Stages of change have been redefined by McNamara (1992, 1998) from the work of Prochaska and Diclemente (1982).

This model can be used by professionals supporting young people in schools primarily to identify how ready, or otherwise, they are for making a change in their behaviour. It is also vital to reinforce the fact that relapsing is part of this process. It is a normal and natural part of the whole cycle of change and young people need to be made aware of this fact and reassured that relapsing does not equate to failure – it simply means that you begin the whole process/cycle again.

It is often useful to adapt the stages of change in order to make them more user friendly for young people and to also provide examples of what someone might say to themselves at each stage in order to further clarify the process. For example:

1 Pre-thinking: the statement might be, 'I don't care if teachers don't like me; I'm really not bothered at all.'

2 Thinking: the statement might be, 'I realise that sometimes the lessons go better when I don't try to get on the teacher's nerves.'

3 Deciding: the statement might be, 'I'm going to try and get on better in more of my lessons so that people feel better about me in general.'

4 Doing: the statement might be, 'I'm working harder now and paying more attention in most of my lessons.'

5   Maintaining: the statement might be, 'I haven't had a detention or a fixed-term exclusion for over six weeks now.'

6   Relapsing: the statement might be, 'I told Mr Francis where to go when he told me I wasn't trying hard enough in my maths project.'

Framework for Developing a Personal Goal

In other approaches to behavioural change young people are often encouraged to identify personal goals, targets and aims for themselves. This is not always done in a SMART (Small, Measurable, Attainable, Relevant, Time-Bound) manner and goals are very rarely separated out into long-term and short-term initiatives. It is also quite unusual to clearly specify the action steps. The MI approach, by contrast, ensures that young people work through this process in a systematic way, stating the problem and identifying long-term and short-term goals and action steps for themselves. The framework is as follows:

1   Reflect on a behaviour you want to change or that you are already working on. Identify a problem area or concern and write a personal goal. Ensure that you use SMART criteria to write your goal, in other words, describe your goal as small, measurable, achievable, realistic and time-bound.

2   State the problem: what is it that you want to do differently? Clarify this. Present the problem in the form of a 'how to' statement.

3   Long-term goal: what would be different in your life if you changed your behaviour and how will you know that things are better for you and others around you?

4   Short-term/SMART goal: this goal must be achievable within 30 days. What would be different over the next few days and weeks if you make this change? What will you be doing or saying differently as a result of the change? What is the greatest barrier to change?

5   Action steps: write down a list of action steps that will be achieved in order to meet the short-term goal. Finally, set a date when you will review this with someone who is important to you and has your best interests at heart.

Objectives of the Programme

The 15 sessions in this programme have been designed to meet the following objectives:

- To increase self-confidence and levels of resilience.

- To increase the use of reframing and positive thinking.

- To enable young people to understand how positive thinking and a positive attitude towards change can minimise stress and anxiety.

- To understand the cycle of change and normalise the relapse element.

- To recognise how we can and should learn from mistakes and failures.

- To recognise when we engage in negative and catastrophising behaviours and thinking.

- To understand the links between thoughts, feelings and behaviours.

- To understand the nature and causes of stress in our lives and how this can be minimized by using tools from CBT.

- To increase cooperation and empathy with others and develop a growth mindset that is outward-focused on others.

- To enable young people to recognise their own optimum stress levels that allow for efficient functioning.

- To understand the concept of ambivalence and the need to work through this in order to identify the changes we want to make in order to promote our well-being.

- To recognise reactions and behaviours that reduce or increase anxiety levels and promote overall well-being.

- To become more autonomous and feel more in control of thoughts, feelings and behaviours in all areas of our lives.

- To understand the importance of emotional support from significant others (friends/family, etc.) in coping effectively with negative thinking.

- To be able to engage in appropriate behavioural experiments that effectively challenge negative thinking patterns and behaviours.

- To understand how a healthy lifestyle can reduce stress and enable us to cope more effectively with a range of problems and still bounce back.

- To develop skills of self-reflection.

- To enable young people to set realistic and considered personal goals that they can and do achieve

About the Programme

This programme is designed to be delivered in whole or in part to individuals, groups and whole classes of children and young people. Each of the 15 sessions follows a similar format and is designed to be delivered in approximately 45 to 60 minutes. Each session includes a series of activities and clear instructions regarding delivery for the teacher or group leader. These are straightforward and transparent in terms of presentation so as to facilitate delivery.

The sessions are arranged as follows:

- Session 1 Thinking about Thinking
- Session 2 NATs & PATs
- Session 3 Doing Yourself Down
- Session 4 Self-Image Issues
- Session 5 What Influences Us?
- Session 6 Core Beliefs & Making the Connections
- Session 7 Beat the Blues
- Session 8 The Change Cycle

Introduction

- Session 9 How to See Failure
- Session 10 Test Your Thinking
- Session 11 My Wants & SMART Targets
- Session 12 Building Positive Thinking Habits
- Session 13 Chillax
- Session 14 Positive Selfie
- Session 15 Reflect, Evaluate & Persist!

The Structure of the Sessions

Apart from Session 1, all the sessions follow a similar format as follows:

Introduction & Aims

To start, reinforce the group rules as agreed in Session 1, and then outline the key aims for the session and briefly summarise the proposed activities.

Warm-Up Activity

Each session will include a warm-up activity, which usually takes the form of a circle-time game and involves the group in tasks that promote social skills development and cooperation. Directions are made explicit in the session plans and are generally very straightforward and easy to follow.

Icebreaker – A Question to Thought-Storm

This question will reflect the main focus of the session and will encourage the group to think more deeply about what they do and don't know and to specifically highlight current knowledge levels and understanding. This will also give you an idea of how much input you may have to give when describing and introducing the key concepts and the activities. The question will be posed by you, and then followed by a group discussion during which you can record contributions (flip chart/whiteboard/interactive whiteboard) and summarise these as appropriate.

Case Study & Questions for Discussion

This part of each session presents the group with a case study. Each study reflects the ineffective thinking that young people can engage in and incorporates scenarios around body image, appearance, self-worth, peer relationships, achievement, motivation, and so on. Pertinent issues are also incorporated within the case studies, including self-harm, sexual objectification, consent and bullying. The subsequent questions are designed to support the development of each person's awareness of such issues alongside their skills in reframing the negative automatic thoughts and in problem-solving a range of key issues and concerns that may have real resonance for them as young people growing up in a complex world.

Activities

The activities (between 3 and 5 per session) are then worked through in turn. These incorporate a range of learning styles and ways of working – pairs, whole group, individually, written, reflections, skills practice, and so on. Clear directions are given in each session plan regarding delivery and key concepts and ideas to be covered.

Feedback & Reflections

This part of the session enables you to ask the group to reflect upon what they have learnt in the session, posing the following questions:

- What was useful to you in this session?

- What might have made the session more useful to you?

- What have you learnt about yourself in today's session?

- What have you learnt about others?

- How will you use your knowledge and skills to help yourself and others in the future?

This is an important element of each session in that it enables the group to really think about what they have learnt and the impact that this may well have upon their overall well-being. Sharing their understanding of the key concepts covered and their own interpretations and learning can also serve to highlight differences and encourage the appreciation of diversity. This process can also highlight and reinforce the strategies and techniques that seem to work for the majority in terms of promoting and maintaining good emotional health.

A Final Thought

We now know that there is an abundant body of research by positive psychologists which shows us that there is not a contradiction between happiness and achievement, and that both are fully embodied in Seligman's (2011) concept of Positive Education. Autonomy support is the process of giving young people a sense of inner independence and thus encouraging their resilience and self-reliance. For the purpose of this programme the distinction between making and encouraging is vital. We can encourage, but we cannot make others flourish.

This programme, therefore, aims to enable young people to understand that happiness and well-being for all of us is at least, in part, about how we think about ourselves and our place in the world. It is not about 'things'. Key messages include the importance of being optimistic and to view ourselves as strong individuals with a sense of purpose. Also, the fact that happiness is at least partly in our heads and some ways of viewing the world make us happier, even if our objective circumstances remain the same. Learning to use key tools of effective thinking supports us in the process of maintaining our well-being and these are the life skills that we can continue to use into adulthood. I sincerely hope that this resource will support young people in this process and provide them with the basis for a really effective well-being tool kit.

Session 1
Thinking about Thinking

Introduction & Aims

In this introductory session it is important to highlight the main purpose and objectives of the programme overall. The focus here is on positive psychology and the development of a healthy and positive mindset in those who will participate in the 15-session programme.

It is therefore important for you to outline that the goal of positive psychology is basically to enhance human strengths such as optimism, courage, honesty, self-understanding and interpersonal skills. This is the opposite of what Dr Martin Seligman calls 'focusing on the broken things and on repairing the damage of past traumas'. Positive psychology provides a means of helping the individual to use inner resources as a buffer against setbacks and adversity in life whenever these crop up. Developing such skills helps to prevent individuals from becoming depressed. As Seligman states, 'It's not about how to heal; it's about to have a great life.'

We know that there is an increase in mental health difficulties in children and young people and that developing a positive mindset and a range of well-being strategies is crucial in preventing the escalation of such difficulties. This is a key objective of the programme as a whole. We know also that positive psychology has to be central to any approach in education in order to achieve such a goal. There is now a wealth of research to confirm that happy people are successful across all domains, including relationships, marriage, longevity, health, income and work performance. Therefore, if we fail to promote this kind of well-being education, we also fail to ensure the optimal functioning and development of young people in our care.

At the outset, highlight the fact that positive psychology can provide all of us with key skills, as follows:

- To continually become aware of our positive experiences.

- To engage in things we enjoy and that give us a buzz.

- To be able to reframe our negative stories and experiences and continually tell ourselves what is positive about our lives.

- To foster flow and aim to remain in that state as much as possible.

- To recall happy memories when we are low.

- To move from our comfort zones to our stretched zones in order to further promote resilience, self-esteem and achievement.

Session 1 Thinking about Thinking

- Not to be frightened to ask for help when we get stressed or find ourselves unable to cope.
- To have the courage to fail and learn from those failures.

You may also wish to outline how the 15 sessions in this programme have been designed to meet the following objectives:

- To increase self-confidence and levels of resilience.
- To increase the use of reframing and positive thinking.
- To enable young people to understand how positive thinking and a positive attitude towards change can minimise stress and anxiety.
- To understand the cycle of change and normalise the relapse element.
- To recognise how we can and should learn from mistakes and failures.
- To recognise when we engage in negative and catastrophising behaviours and thinking.
- To understand the links between thoughts, feelings and behaviours.
- To understand the nature and causes of stress in our lives and how this can be minimised by using tools from CBT.
- To increase cooperation and empathy with others and develop a growth mindset that is outward-focused on others.
- To enable young people to recognise their own optimum stress levels that allow for efficient functioning.
- To understand the concept of ambivalence and the need to work through this in order to identify the changes we want to make in order to promote our well-being.
- To recognise reactions and behaviours that both reduce or increase anxiety levels and promote overall well-being.
- To become more autonomous and feel more in control of thoughts, feelings and behaviours in all areas of our lives.
- To understand the importance of emotional support from significant others (friends/ family, etc.) in coping effectively with negative thinking.
- To be able to engage in appropriate behavioural experiments that effectively challenge negative thinking patterns and behaviours.
- To understand how a healthy lifestyle can reduce stress and enable us to cope more effectively with a range of problems and still bounce back.
- To develop skills of self-reflection.
- To enable young people to set realistic and considered personal goals that they can and do achieve.

In this first session, the group will be encouraged to formulate group rules, and to consider the importance of developing and maintaining a positive outlook and how this can impact upon our mental health. Attitudes towards mental health difficulties and the notion of stigmatising such problems will also be covered alongside some of the key myths and realities around these issues. The importance of teaching helpful skills and strategies from positive psychology will also be addressed via a recent newspaper article. Developing happier thinking habits is clearly a crucial aspect of such a process and will, of course, permeate the subsequent sessions of the programme.

Setting Ground Rules

You will need to emphasise the importance of setting appropriate ground rules in order to ensure that everyone can contribute and feel safe and secure within the group. If the group have difficulty in identifying rules at the outset, it may be helpful to provide them with some ideas. Your ideas sheet can be photocopied and distributed, as group members may wish to read through the ideas and select the ones that they feel most appropriate. Once decided, record your agreed ground rules on paper and let everyone have a copy; this can be enlarged to A3 size, if necessary. Alternatively, ground rules can be recorded on the flip chart or whiteboard. The ideas sheet for ground rules may include the following:

- It is important that we listen to each other and show each other respect.
- We shouldn't judge each other or put each other down.
- We need to be tolerant and not think ourselves in any sense superior to someone else or their culture.
- We need to empathise and think about other people's feelings in the group.
- We need to keep things confidential to the group alone and not talk about them outside of the room.
- We shouldn't put each other down.
- We can pass on an activity or discussion if we need to.

It is important that you reinforce the fact that each person needs to agree to the rules and needs to adhere to them throughout the remaining sessions. It will be important to also emphasise the fact that if group members do break any of the rules then this will naturally mean that the individual concerned will be challenged about their responses or behaviours. The ground rules can clearly be reinforced at the start of every subsequent session.

Warm-Up Activity

This initial warm-up activity requires the group to sit as for circle time and then change places around the circle if the following can be said to be true:

- You are wearing something red.
- You are feeling happy today.
- You are feeling rather down today.
- You are wearing something blue.
- You had a positive experience last week.
- You had a negative experience last week, and so on.

Session 1   Thinking about Thinking

Once group members have engaged in the moving around activity, they can then be split into pairs and asked to identify three things that they have in common with their partner. One of the partners can then feed these common elements back to the rest of the group. The aim is to break down any embarrassments or initial barriers in order to ensure that group members can feel relaxed with one another and begin to communicate in a more natural and less guarded manner.

Icebreaker – A Question to Thought-Storm

The group can be asked to focus upon a key question in order to prompt thinking and awareness around some of the most important issues to be covered in this session. It will be essential to encourage everyone to participate and generate their own responses, but also to ensure that everyone feels safe in doing so. The responses can be recorded on a whiteboard or flip chart, as appropriate, and you can also highlight any similarities and differences in the responses. The idea is to begin to encourage a deeper level of thinking around the key issues via the process of cooperative idea-sharing.

The key question for this session is: Is a positive outlook something that we are born with or can we develop this over time?

Case Study & Questions for Discussion

Michael has been having some very negative thoughts about himself for some time now and these are really beginning to get him down. His mum has been diagnosed with depression and has been finding it hard to get to work and do all the usual things like cook their meals and sort the washing, so he and his sister have had to take on more of the chores. He is finding this hard as he also has far more pressure on him at school with revising for his mock exams. He worries about not being able to fit in time for studying and that he will fail as there is just too much to do and he is really feeling overwhelmed. Deep inside, he just wishes that he could opt out and stay at home with his mum, as he worries about her so much when he is at school that this stops him from concentrating and getting on with the work in lessons anyway. He keeps getting into a negative cycle of thinking that he can't do the work because of these pressures, so therefore he doesn't bother and then he gets into trouble and the teachers say he's lazy – so he just thinks that he should give up as they have labelled him now and whatever he does he will not be able to change their opinion of him.

- What kind of thoughts do you think Michael is having?
- What are the main pressures?
- How might his mother's illness be affecting him?
- Is he right about the teacher's opinions of him? Where is the evidence for this?
- If you were his friend, what advice would you give him?
- How can he break this cycle and where can he get the best help?

Activities

1.1   An Article for Discussion

Give everyone a copy of Worksheet 1.1, which contains an article in which a new initiative is described. It involves pupils who are piloting a new well-being scheme in their schools with the aim of promoting well-being and teaching young people a range of skills and strategies from positive psychology. The rationale for doing so is presented in terms of the rise in teenage depression rates, with the average age for the first signs of depression now being 14 ½ years old, whereas it was almost 30 years old half a century ago.

The article focuses on the work of US-based psychologist Dr Martin Seligman who says that lessons in happiness should be on the school curriculum in order to try to improve young people's mental health.

Seligman's ideas of 'positive education' are now being tested in schools in Manchester, south Tyneside and Hertfordshire. Pupils are being taught how to handle day-to-day stress, assertiveness, and decision-making and how to change negative thoughts.

Ask the group to discuss the article and to consider whether it might have any relevance for them and for their school. Would this type of programme be useful or relevant? Would they see this as something that might or could help them?

1.2   Mental Health – Myths & Realities

Worksheet 1.2 contains a series of statements about mental health. Ask the group to consider whether they are true or false. This myths and realities exercise is intended to generate debate and prompt them to think in more depth about these issues. You could begin by reading the statements to the group and asking them to consider each in turn before you give them the worksheet, which details the 'right' responses.

1.3   The Well-Being Checklist

The checklist on Worksheet 1.3 is intended to provide group members with an opportunity to reflect on their own well-being and to identify how well they are currently feeling about their mental health and how they are managing to look after themselves. Ask them to tick the statements that they feel most accurately describe them at this current time. It is important that the group to have time to do this in a confidential way and to also have access to you or another appropriate person should any issues arise from this activity.

1.4   The Negative Internal Monologue

Worksheet 1.4 will help to generate discussion about what negative internal monologues mean for us as individuals. Ask the group to think about how easy it is to get stuck in such a cycle of negative thinking and how one negative thought can so easily lead to another. They may wish to focus on identifying how they might get out of such a cycle. What would they need to do in terms of changing their thinking and behaviour patterns? Who might help them in this process?

1.5   Self-Fulfilling Prophecies

Worksheet 1.5 outlines the concept of the self-fulfilling prophecy in diagram form and will help to generate further discussion. Explain to the group that there are four key principles:

- We form certain expectations of people or events.

- We communicate those expectations with various cues.

- People tend to respond to these cues by adjusting their behaviour to match them.

- The result is that the original expectation becomes true; this creates a circle of self-fulfilling prophecies.

Ask the group to identify times when they know that they have engaged in such a pattern of thinking and to discuss these with a partner or within the group as a whole – whichever seems to be most appropriate and useful.

Feedback & Reflections

Ask the group to reflect upon what they have learnt in the session, posing the following questions:

- What was useful for you in this session?

- What might have made the session more useful for you?

- What have you learnt about yourself in today's session?

- What have you learnt about others?

- How will you use your knowledge and skills to help yourself and others in the future?

The aim is to ensure that the group are able to reflect upon their knowledge and skills and also specifically to identify how and when they might transfer these into new situations in the future.

1.1 An Article for Discussion

Read the article below and think about whether this idea might have any relevance for you and your school. Do you think this type of programme would be useful or relevant? Do you think this is something that might or could help you?

Call for happiness lessons as teenage depression increases

Society Guardian, Wednesday 10 September 2008

Pupils in Manchester, where well-being classes have been piloted.

Photograph: Howard Walker/Manchester Evening News Syndication

The number of teenagers showing signs of depression has risen dramatically over the last 50 years, a mental health expert has revealed.

The average age for the first signs of depression is now 14½, whereas it was almost 30 half a century ago.

US-based psychologist Dr Martin Seligman says lessons in happiness should be on the school curriculum to try to improve young people's mental health.

Speaking at a conference in London yesterday, Seligman said a $2.8m (£1.6m), three-year study in the United States found that children who had been taught 'positive psychology' performed better in class. Teachers also reported these young people had higher social skills and were more engaged.

'The evidence is that well-being is synergistic with traditional learning: people who are in positive states learn better,' he told the conference, organised by the Young Foundation and its local wellbeing project.

Seligman's ideas of 'positive education' are now being tested in schools in Manchester, south Tyneside and Hertfordshire. Pupils are being taught how to handle day-to-day stress, assertiveness, decision-making and how to change negative thoughts.

He told the audience of social care workers, local authority staff, educationalists and exclusion specialists the pupils have a significantly lower rate of conduct disorder, anxiety and depression.

Irene Lucas, the chief executive of South Tyneside council, said the wellbeing project has had such a positive impact on young people, it was as though 'pixie dust and magic' had been sprinkled on an area where over half of the residents live in wards which rank in the country's most deprived 25%.

Well-being and happiness are being taken seriously by ministers. The work and pensions secretary, James Purnell, told the conference: 'Well-being has gone from being a new and interesting idea to becoming a mainstream idea in policy, embraced by politicians of all stripes.'

1.2 Mental Health - Myths & Realities

Statement	Myth or Reality	Explanation
Mental health problems are rare	MYTH	Mental health problems affect one in four people in any one year. So even if you don't have a mental health problem, it's likely your best friend, a family member or work colleague will be affected.
People with mental health problems are often violent	MYTH	People with mental health problems are much more likely to be the victims of violence. This myth makes it harder for people to talk openly about mental health problems. It can also make friends reluctant to stay in touch.
People can't work if they have a mental health problem	MYTH	With one in four people affected by mental health problems, you probably work with someone with a mental health problem.
People with mental health problems never recover	MYTH	Many people can and do recover completely from mental health problems. Alongside professional help, the support of friends, family and getting back to work are all important in helping people recover.
Other people can't tell if you have a mental health problem	REALITY	Mental health problems are as real as a broken arm, although there isn't a sling or plaster cast to show for it. Many of those who are affected deal with it alone as nobody else knows.
On average, people who experience mental health problems don't live as long	REALITY	However, it's not the mental health problem that's responsible. The physical health needs of people with mental health problems are often dismissed, causing higher rates of death from heart attacks, diabetes and cancer, for people with severe mental illness.
We all have mental health, like we all have physical health	REALITY	Just like our physical health, our mental health will vary from time to time and it is important that we take care of both.
People with mental health problems often experience discrimination	REALITY	Nine out of ten people with mental health problems experience stigma and discrimination.

1.3 The Well-Being Checklist

Read the statements below and tick the statements you feel most accurately describe YOU!

You don't have to share your answers with any other group members: this is your private checklist.

1   I would describe myself as:

a   Quite a happy and content person who can cope with life's ups and downs.

b   Rather a serious person who worries a bit, but is relatively contented.

c   Upset, agitated and irritable for most of the time.

2   I generally feel that:

a   Good things tend to happen to me and I'm hopeful about my future.

b   I find myself worrying quite a lot about the future.

c   I have few choices in my life and things are more likely to get worse than better in the future.

3   I would describe myself as:

a   Sociable and confident, with lots of good friends.

b   Sometimes finding it hard to talk to my friends – especially when things are difficult.

c   Not having many close friends and sometimes not knowing where to turn.

4   Generally, I would cry:

a   If something happened that made me feel very sad.

b   Relatively easily, as I can be a little sensitive sometimes.

c   Very easily and often I will cry without knowing why.

5   Mostly my sleep is:

a   Good and I wake up feeling refreshed and energised.

b   Quite good, but sometimes I find it hard to get to sleep and I wake up early.

c   Disturbed, because I don't sleep well or for long enough or I sleep all the time. I don't want to get out of bed in the mornings and simply want to pull the covers over my head and stay there.

6   When I have a lot going on in my life:

a   I try and keep a balance and still see my friends or do other things I enjoy.

b   My friendships and social activities tend to suffer.

c   I hide myself away.

Page 1 of 2

How did you do?

Mostly A's

You are able to look after yourself well and know when and how to get help. You can talk about your feelings and make sure that you keep a balance between work and social activities. You just need to keep monitoring yourself and setting realistic targets in order to maintain your well-being. You can also try to learn new strategies from this programme in order to maintain and further develop positive thinking.

Mostly B's

You sometimes feel overwhelmed and don't take care of your emotional and physical needs. You need to make a well-being plan for yourself, identifying strategies to keep well and others who can help you. This needs to include keeping an eye on personal stress and using stress-busting techniques. Developing more effective thinking processes will be key for you, so hopefully you will be able to learn some of the key tools and strategies by participating in this programme.

Mostly C's

You are finding life difficult and feel overwhelmed for the majority of the time. You need to talk about these problems with a mentor/counsellor and start to develop some self-help strategies. Visit 'Top tips for positive mental health' (www.wellscotland.info/top tips) and begin to make a plan. This programme will also provide you with relevant information and opportunities to develop self-help skills and the tools you need to develop and maintain more effective thinking. Go for it!

Note: If completing this worksheet has made you feel that you would like to speak to someone privately about any of the issues, your group leader will be able to help you.

Page 2 of 2

1.4 The Negative Internal Monologue

Think about how easy it is to get stuck in a cycle of negative thinking and how one negative thought can so easily lead to another.

Try to focus on thinking of ways of getting out of such a cycle.

- What would you need to do in terms of changing your thinking and behaviour patterns to get out of the cycle?

- Who might help you in this process?

I am so far behind, I may as well give up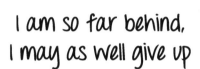

I am stupid

Nobody cares

I can't do it

I am a failure

1.5 Self-Fulfilling Prophecies

The diagram below shows how a self-fulfilling prophecy works. There are four key stages:

1   We form certain expectations of people or events.

2   We communicate those expectations with various cues.

3   People tend to respond to these cues by adjusting their behaviour to match them.

4   The result is that the original expectation becomes true; this creates a circle of self-fulfilling prophecy.

Try to think of times when you have engaged in such a pattern of thinking and discuss these with a partner or within the whole group.

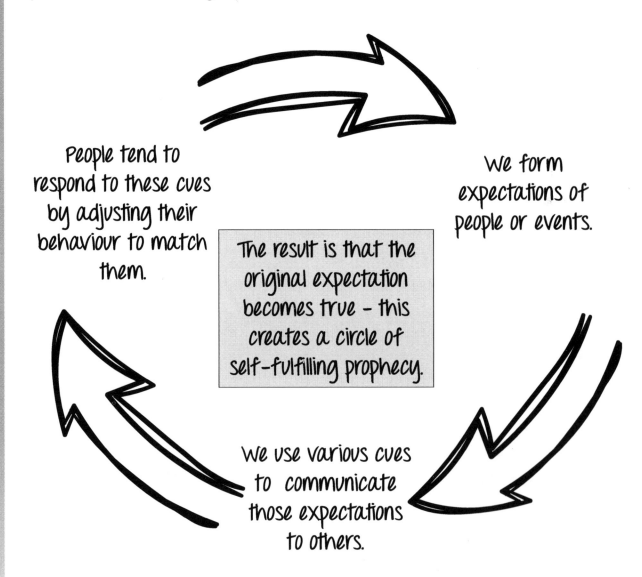

People tend to respond to these cues by adjusting their behaviour to match them.

We form expectations of people or events.

The result is that the original expectation becomes true – this creates a circle of self-fulfilling prophecy.

We use various cues to communicate those expectations to others.

Session 2
NATs & PATs

Introduction & Aims

In this session the group are asked to focus upon their thinking and to specifically consider how we may engage in negative patterns of thinking on a regular basis and how this may often be a counterproductive experience for us.

The key aims are as follows:

- The group are introduced to and gain a basic understanding of the therapeutic approach known as Cognitive Behavioural Therapy (CBT), which is a set of tools to help us deal more effectively with our problems and find the best solutions to them.

- They are asked to look at the links between thoughts, feelings and behaviours and to understand how easy it is to get into a negative cycle of thinking, feeling and behaving.

- Group members are asked to consider the statement, 'How you think about something will become true,' and to consider how we can change the way that we think and become more effective thinkers in order to gain more control over our lives. The aim is to ensure that they can and do recognise that we can all learn more effective thinking skills.

- They are finally given the opportunity to identify personal negative and positive automatic thoughts they have at this point in time.

Warm-up Activity

This warm-up activity is entitled 'Who are you?' Collect a selection of pictures of famous people, such as pop stars, television personalities, film stars, and so on. Tape one to each person's back without them seeing the picture. The group can now walk around the room and question others about the character in their picture – without actually asking for the name – until each person is able to guess the character on their back. It may be necessary to repeat and reinforce the initial group rules at this point in the session. Once everyone has guessed their character, ask the group to form a circle and consider the following question: 'What do you feel about your character and why?'

Icebreaker - A Question to Thought-Storm

The group can be asked to focus upon a key question in order to prompt thinking and awareness around some of the most important issues to be covered in this session. It will be essential to encourage everyone to participate and generate their own responses, but also to ensure that everyone feels safe in doing so. The responses can be recorded on a whiteboard or flip chart, as appropriate, and you can also highlight any similarities and differences in the responses. The idea is to begin to encourage a deeper level of thinking around the key issues via the process of cooperative idea-sharing.

The key question for this session is: Do human beings generally have more negative thoughts than positive ones on a daily basis and, if so, what does this suggest for their overall well-being?

Case Study & Questions for Discussion

Keiron has got himself into a negative cycle of thinking. He has recurring thoughts that he just can't be a success. He thinks that however hard he tries he will not be able to manage the workload he has at school and will ultimately fail. This isn't good as it means that he has closed down and stopped talking to his friends and family who had been very supportive of him. He just can't seem to get the thought out of his head that he is going to fail and that he is useless. His dad has told him to get a grip and just grow up. This hasn't been helpful to him.

- What kind of thoughts do you think Keiron is having?
- Where do you think these thoughts come from?
- What are the main pressures that he may be experiencing?
- How might his father's attitude be affecting him?
- Is he right in believing that he will ultimately fail? Where is the evidence for this?
- If you were his friend, what advice would you give him?
- How can he break this negative cycle and how do you think he can help himself?

Activities

2.1   What is Cognitive Behavioural Therapy or CBT?

Give each group member a copy of Worksheet 2.1, which briefly introduces Cognitive Behavioural Therapy (CBT) as a set of tools that will help people to deal with problems and find the best solutions. The following description can be read to the group to help explain this further.

Cognitive Behavioural Therapy (CBT) focuses on the role that thoughts play in relation to both our emotions and our behaviours. This approach advocates that change in thought processes can have a significant effect upon altering behaviours. Unlike many of the talking treatments that traditional therapists have used, CBT focuses upon the 'here and now', as well as ways to improve the individual's state of mind in the present time. This is innovative in the sense that there is no focus on the causes of distress or past symptoms as there evidently is with traditional psychotherapy.

Restructuring thought processes

Young people are frequently flooded with anxious and negative thoughts and doubts. These messages will often reinforce a state of inadequacy and/or low levels of self-esteem. The process of CBT helps to support young people in reconsidering these negative assumptions. It also allows them to learn how to change their self-perceptions in order to improve their mental and emotional state – this is the key aim of this kind of intervention. Changing negative thought patterns or opinions will ultimately help young people to become more able to control and change their behaviours, but this does take practice. This is why, as with anger management interventions, another key element of the approach is the requirement to learn, and to put into practice, the skills or strategies discussed in any session.

2.2   Looking at the Links

Worksheet 2.2 explains the way in which the CBT approach breaks a particular problem into stages A, B and C. Explain to the group the process as follows:

- **A**, the **activating event**, is often referred to as the 'trigger' – the thing that causes you to engage in the negative thinking.

- **B** represents these negative **beliefs**, which can include thoughts, rules and demands, and the meanings the individual attaches to both external and internal events.

- **C** is the **consequences** or emotions, and the behaviours and physical sensations accompanying these different emotions. It is important to highlight and discuss with the group how the way that they think about a problem can affect how they feel physically and emotionally. It can also alter what they do about it. This is why the key aim for CBT is to break the negative, vicious cycle that some people may find themselves in. For example, if you think that you will get your work wrong you feel angry, and then you do not give it a try in case it is wrong.

2.3   Breaking the Cycle

In this activity the group are asked to consider how identifying our Negative Automatic Thoughts (NATs) is the first step in learning how to feel and be a positive person. Give everyone a copy of Worksheet 2.3 and discuss the cycle shown. Now ask each person to try to identify a NAT that they have recently had, working through the cycle and identifying their thoughts and feelings and behaviours at each stage.

2.4   NATs & PATs!

Worksheet 2.4 will help the group to think about both Negative and Positive Automatic Thoughts (NATs and PATs). Working in pairs, ask the group to use the worksheet to think about and identify NATs and PATs that they have about themselves and their futures. Discuss with partners similarities and differences in their thinking patterns.

Feedback & Reflections

Ask the group to reflect upon what they have learnt in the session, posing the following questions:

- What was useful for you in this session?
- What might have made the session more useful for you?
- What have you learnt about yourself in today's session?
- What have you learnt about others?
- How will you use your knowledge and skills to help yourself and others in the future?

The aim is to ensure that the group are able to reflect upon their knowledge and skills and also specifically to identify how and when they might transfer these into new situations in the future.

2.1 What is Cognitive Behavioural Therapy or CBT?

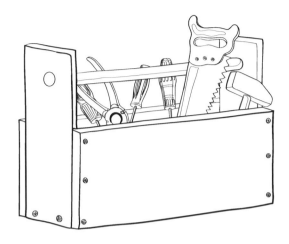

CBT is a set of tools
to help you deal with problems
and find the best solutions.

Looking at Links ...

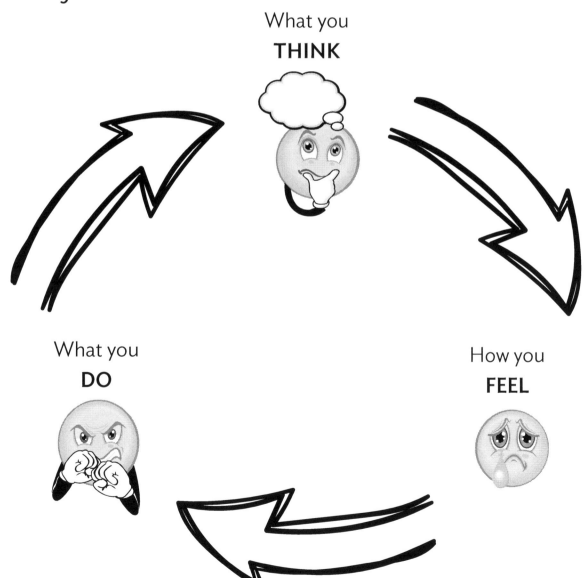

What you
THINK

How you
FEEL

What you
DO

2.2 Looking at the Links

The table below explains the way in which the CBT approach breaks a particular problem into three smaller parts.

How do these links work?

Think ...	Feel ...	Do ...
I'm useless at meeting new people.	I feel scared and nervous when I meet new people.	I don't talk to them and go quiet.
No one in my year likes me.	I feel sad and angry.	I avoid going out at break and start to bunk off school.
I'm rubbish at maths.	I feel dumb and fed up.	I stop trying because I know I'll get it all wrong.

Statement: **How you think about something will become the truth.**

STOP, THINK & REFLECT

- Is this statement true?
- Can we change the way we think?
- Can we handle our problems differently to change how we feel and what we do?
- Can we gain more *control* over what happens to us in our lives?

2.3 Breaking the Cycle

The diagram below shows how Negative Automatic Thoughts (NATs) develop.
Try to think of a NAT that you have had recently and work through the cycle, thinking about your thoughts, feelings and behaviours at each stage.

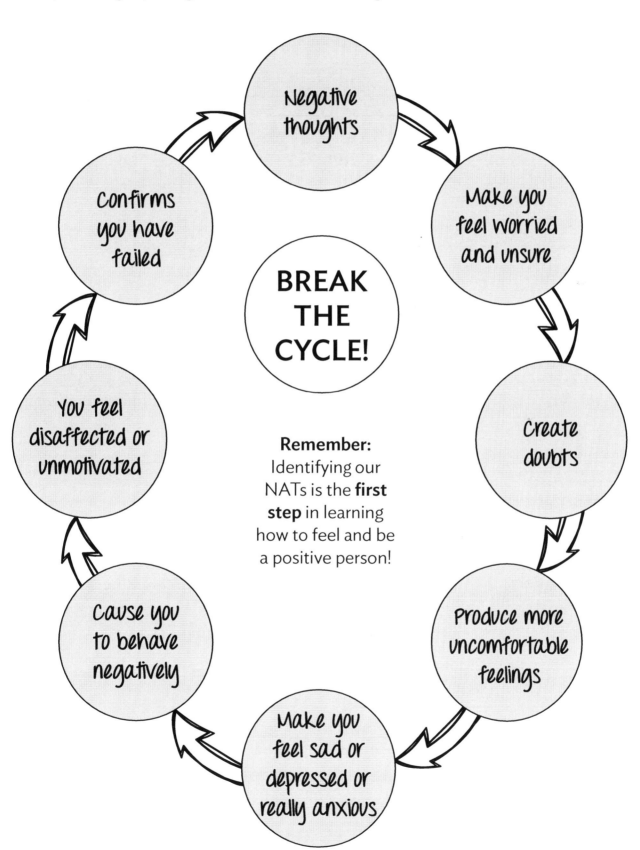

Negative thoughts

Make you feel worried and unsure

Create doubts

Produce more uncomfortable feelings

Make you feel sad or depressed or really anxious

Cause you to behave negatively

You feel disaffected or unmotivated

Confirms you have failed

BREAK THE CYCLE!

Remember: Identifying our NATs is the **first step** in learning how to feel and be a positive person!

2.4 NATs & PATs!

Work with a partner to think about and identify Positive and Negative Automatic Thoughts that you have about yourself and your future. Write them in the boxes below.

PATs (Positive Automatic Thoughts) What positive thoughts do you have?	NATs (Negative Automatic Thoughts) What negative thoughts to you have?
(A) ABOUT YOU	**(B)** ABOUT YOU
(C) ABOUT YOUR FUTURE	**(D)** ABOUT YOUR FUTURE

Session 3

Doing Yourself Down

Introduction & Aims

In this session the group are asked to focus further upon their thinking and to specifically consider how we may all engage in putting both ourselves and others down and how this may often be a counterproductive experience for us, resulting in negative outcomes.

The key aims are as follows:

- For the group to consider why we may want, or seem to need to want, to put others down and also to put ourselves down and negate any of our successes.

- To consider the key influences in our lives and the feelings that these generate – both positive and negative – and to begin to consider how our core beliefs about ourselves are linked to the ways in which others have treated us and the messages that they have given to us over time.

- For the group to begin to identify their own core beliefs and begin to consider how these may impact upon their behaviours in the social and learning context. Making the distinction between the beliefs that are helpful and unhelpful to them is key in this process.

- For the group to begin to understand and engage in the process of challenging Unhelpful Assumptions/Rules – another key to developing effective thinking.

Warm-up Activity

This warm-up activity is entitled 'What am I?' Ask the group to sit in a circle and to then take a minute or so to think about the activities they most enjoy outside of school. Now ask group members to change places if:

- You like doing a sporting activity (for example, playing football).
- You like shopping.
- You like staying in.
- You like playing computer games.
- You like cooking, and so on.

Session 3   Doing Yourself Down

Once everyone has changed places, give each person one activity card, face down. Now tell everyone that they can look at their card, but not show it to anyone else. Take a card for yourself and explain that each person has to describe or act out the profession marked on the card. This can be done using words or actions, but they cannot use the word marked on the card. Use your own card to demonstrate. Simple props, such as a chair, may be used and the 'actor' may stay at his/her place or come to the middle of the circle.

Once the group have guessed the profession correctly, ask the actor: '[Name], do you think you could be a [name of professional]? What qualities do you think you need to be a good [name of professional]?

Icebreaker – A Question to Thought-Storm

The group can be asked to focus upon a key question in order to prompt thinking and awareness around some of the most important issues to be covered in this session. It will be essential to encourage everyone to participate and generate their own responses, but also to ensure that everyone feels safe in doing so. The responses can be recorded on a whiteboard or flip chart, as appropriate, and you can also highlight any similarities and differences in the responses. The idea is to begin to encourage a deeper level of thinking around the key issues via the process of cooperative idea-sharing.

The key question for this session is: Why do people put each other down and how can we deal with such behaviour?

Case Study & Questions for Discussion

Ella is always doing herself down and telling herself that she is not good enough. She thinks that all her friends are prettier, more popular and thinner than she is and that she will never get a boyfriend because she isn't as good looking as the rest of them. Last week there was a party at her friend's house and she was the only one who didn't get a dance or chatted up by any of the boys. She felt really down about it, so went off and sulked in the toilet. She felt that it was just all so unfair and only happening to her since everyone else seemed to be having such a good time.

- What kind of thoughts do you think Ella is having?
- What are the main pressures?
- How might her attitude influence her friendships and the ways she responds to others?
- Is she right in thinking that everyone else is having such a good time? Where is the evidence for this?
- If you were her friend, what advice would you give her?
- How can she break this cycle and what could she do to help herself?

Activities

3.1 Influences & Feelings

Using Worksheet 3.1, ask the group to list the main places, people and activities in their lives and then think about and write down the feelings that go with each of these. This will help to reinforce the fact that some people, and some situations or events, may produce less positive feelings and responses than others. This can be due to the behaviour of others and the ways in which we choose to respond to them. It is important that we can and do reflect upon such events and contexts so that we can begin to reduce the negative influences and experiences in our lives and to learn how to manage these more effectively.

3.2 Who are You? What do You Believe?

It is vital that we are conscious of our personal belief systems and the core beliefs that we have about ourselves. Ask the group to write down 10 things they believe about themselves on Worksheet 3.2. This task should be completed relatively quickly so that group members do not have time to change the beliefs about themselves that simply pop into their heads straight away. Such first thoughts are more likely to be what people really think and feel so it may be helpful for you to place a time limit on this part of the activity.

Now ask the group to think about the following questions and then share their responses in the whole group:

- How do your beliefs make you FEEL?
- How do your beliefs affect how you ACT?
- Do NEGATIVE core beliefs set you up to fail and limit what you do?

3.3 The 'If ... & Then' Task – Your Core Beliefs

Using Worksheet 3.3, ask everyone to complete the sentence starters in order to further reflect upon and identify their core beliefs.

Once completed, give everyone time to think about and discuss their answers in order to identify those beliefs that may or may not be helpful. This is very important, as knowing which beliefs are unhelpful and understanding how we can move forward from these and change or redirect our thinking is the next vital step in maintaining and further developing effective thinking.

3.4 Challenging Unhelpful Beliefs & Rules

The final activity in this session is intended to build upon and reinforce the previous ones and to encourage the group to identify the specific advantages of holding or not holding on to their core beliefs and assumptions. Making use of such a strategy is clearly helpful and can become part of their repertoire of effective thinking skills in the future.

Using Worksheet 3.4, ask everyone to think of one of their core beliefs about themselves, and then to list both the advantages and disadvantages of holding on to this belief.

Feedback & Reflections

Ask the group to reflect upon what they have learnt in the session, posing the following questions:

- ◼ What was useful for you in this session?

- ◼ What might have made the session more useful for you?

- ◼ What have you learnt about yourself in today's session?

- ◼ What have you learnt about others?

- ◼ How will you use your knowledge and skills to help yourself and others in the future?

The aim is to ensure that the group are able to reflect upon their knowledge and skills and also specifically to identify how and when they might transfer these into new situations in the future.

Session 3   Doing Yourself Down

3.1 Influences & Feelings

In the spaces below, list the main places, people and activities in your life. Then think about and write down the feelings that go with each of these.

Place/Person/Activity	Feelings

3.2 Who are You? What do You Believe?

Without taking too much time think, write down the first 10 things about yourself that come into your head.

1	I think I am
2	I think I am
3	I think I am
4	I think I am
5	I think I am
6	I think I am
7	I think I am
8	I think I am
9	I think I am
10	I think I am

STOP, THINK & REFLECT

- How do your beliefs make you FEEL?
- How do your beliefs affect how you ACT?
- Do NEGATIVE core beliefs set you up to fail and limit what you do?

3.3 The 'If ... & Then' Task - Your Core Beliefs

Have a go at completing these statements. What do you think will happen in each situation? Stop, think & reflect and then TALK it through.

IF _____, THEN _____

If I am bad, then _____

If I get it wrong, then _____

If I work hard, then _____

If I am kind, then _____

If I have friends, then _____

If I am good, then _____

If I make people feel good, then _____

If I don't have friends, then _____

If I let people down, then _____

If I think positively, then _____

Which beliefs are helpful? _____

Why? _____

_____

Which beliefs are unhelpful? _____

Why? _____

_____

3.4 Challenging Unhelpful Beliefs & Rules

Write down one of your core beliefs about yourself below and then think about and list all of the advantages and also the disadvantages of holding on to this belief. Try to remember this exercise and to use it at other times to examine some of your other beliefs.

My Core Belief or Rule _____

Advantages of holding this belief or rule	Disadvantages of holding this belief or rule

Session 4

Self-Image Issues

Introduction 4 Aims

In this session the focus is primarily on supporting the group to recognise their strengths and to particularly develop the ability to engage in cognitive reframing. This is specifically related to self-image issues, which are, of course, particularly relevant to adolescents.

The key aims are as follows:

- For group members to be able to identify what influences the way we feel about our looks and self-image; to further be able to consider and identify if these influences always helpful/positive.

- To provide an opportunity to challenge our negative thoughts and check out the evidence identifying how true are these thoughts and how we can change negative thoughts into more balanced thoughts.

- To gain confidence in reframing NATs.

- To understand how keeping a positive mindset involves hard work and dedication and that focusing on the positives on a daily basis can help us to keep a more balanced perspective.

- To introduce the concept of Socratic questioning, using a simple 'and so' strategy; for group members to see how this can be useful in challenging their four most common automatic thoughts.

Warm-Up Activity

The aim of this activity is for the group to recognise that they all have an area of strength and that this may be different from that of their peers. You can choose from one of the following two activities:

1   In a circle, ask each person to completes the sentence, 'I am good at ...'

2   Ask group members to swap places 'if ...', for example, they can play a musical instrument/ sing/know another language/ride a horse, and so on.

Icebreaker – A Question to Thought-Storm

The group can be asked to focus upon a key question in order to prompt thinking and awareness around some of the most important issues to be covered in this session. It will be essential to encourage everyone to participate and generate their own responses, but also to ensure that everyone feels safe in doing so. The responses can be recorded on a whiteboard or flip chart, as appropriate, and you can also highlight any similarities and differences in the responses. The idea is to begin to encourage a deeper level of thinking around the key issues via the process of cooperative idea-sharing.

The key question for this session is: What influences the way we feel about our looks and self-image and are these influences always helpful/positive?

Case Study 4 Questions for Discussion

Callum has an issue with how he looks. He feels that he has such a puny body and that he isn't as tall or well-built as the other boys in his year group. They call him the wimp (along with lots of other things that simply can't be repeated here). He is getting really fed up about this, but also increasingly self-conscious as he feels that he will never be accepted in the group and will also always be the one that no one fancies. He wants to look like David Beckham so spends hours in his room doing his weights, but that doesn't seem to be making any difference to his body size and shape at all. His mum thinks he's just being stupid and constantly tells him just to be patient and that he will grow – he just has to wait another couple of years.

- What kind of thoughts do you think Callum is having?
- What are the main pressures?
- How might his mother's comments be affecting him and how useful do you think that they are?
- If you were his friend, what advice would you give him?
- How can he break this cycle and where can he get the best advice?

Activities

4.1   Problem Scenario

This activity reinforces the problems we may encounter when our 'friends' put us down or make negative comments about us and the choices that we can make about how we respond to such behaviours. Worksheet 4.1 contains a short scenario. Read this out to the group and then ask everyone to think about answers to the questions.

Janis has always been worried about her weight and it doesn't help that her best friend is really slim and is always noticed by the boys. So, recently, Janis has become more interested in her appearance and she has begun to buy fashion and celebrity magazines. She spends a lot of time looking at the possible outfits that she could buy and admiring the slim bodies of the models and celebrities.

One day while she is spending time with her best friend, Emily, Janis shows her some of the clothes she was thinking about buying in the magazines. Emily giggles and jokes, 'You can't wear that – your stomach will be hanging over!'

- What are the different ways in which Janis could react to that comment?
- Do you think that Emily cares about Janis' weight?
- Is there some different way in which Emily could have worded her statement?
- Does Janis feel ugly?
- In which ways could Janis improve the way she feels about herself (self-esteem)?
- What should Janis do now that she knows what her friend thinks about her?
- Is Emily a good friend?

Ask the group to begin by working in pairs and then to discuss their responses in the whole group while you act as a scribe and highlight any similarities and differences in their thinking. It is important to highlight that our responses are effectively a choice and that we can choose to respond in both helpful and unhelpful ways to this kind of bullying or unkindness.

4.2   Reframe It!

In this activity the group are given further opportunities to practise their skills of reframing thoughts and beliefs. We should always challenge our negative thoughts or beliefs and should always examine the evidence. Using Worksheet 4.2, ask everyone to think about how true a series of negative thoughts might be and how someone might change these from negative thoughts into more balanced thoughts. On the worksheet they should have a go at reframing these NATs (the first one is done for them). Once the task is completed, ask the whole group to share responses that people might find useful in order to stimulate new ideas and suggestions.

4.3   My List of Positives

This is an important activity in that it presents the group with an easy and practical task they can continue to use in supporting their overall well-being and reinforcing the positives in their lives. Sometimes we forget to think about the positive or good things that happen and this is not healthy. Ask group members to keep a log of positives during the coming week. Every evening ask them to think of one thing (at least) that has happened which made them feel good and to record this on the positive scroll on Worksheet 4.3. At the end of the week they can look at their list and this will help to reinforce that positive things really do happen to them.

4.4   Four Big NATs

Using Worksheet 4.4, ask the group to identify their four most common automatic thoughts (those they have most often on a daily basis) and to then make use of the 'and so' strategy: '... and so, if this were true, what would it say about me?' Explain that this type of Socratic questioning should begin to help them to see that some of their thinking errors are not entirely rational and that when we begin to delve further and challenge such thoughts we can also begin to see how illogical they are and how they are not based on real and tangible evidence.

Feedback & Reflections

Ask the group to reflect upon what they have learnt in the session, posing the following questions:

- What was useful for you in this session?

- What might have made the session more useful for you?

- What have you learnt about yourself in today's session?

- What have you learnt about others?

- How will you use your knowledge and skills to help yourself and others in the future?

The aim is to ensure that the group are able to reflect upon their knowledge and skills and also specifically to identify how and when they might transfer these into new situations in the future.

Session 4 Self-Image Issues

4.1 Problem Scenario

Working with a partner, carefully read the story below, and then think about your answers to the questions. In the whole group discuss your answers and think about the similarities and differences in the ways people have answered.

> Janis has always been worried about her weight and it doesn't help that her best friend is really slim and is always noticed by the boys.
>
> So recently, Janis has become more interested in her appearance and she has begun to buy fashion and celebrity magazines. She spends a lot of time looking at the possible outfits that she could buy and admiring the slim bodies of the models and celebrities.
>
> One day while she is spending time with her best friend, Emily, Janis shows her some of the clothes she was thinking about buying in the magazines. Emily giggles and jokes, 'You can't wear that – your stomach will be hanging over!'

- What are the different ways in which Janis could react to that comment?
- Do you think that Emily cares about Janis' weight?
- Is there some different way in which Emily could have worded her statement?
- Does Janis feel ugly?
- In which ways could Janis improve the way she feels about herself (self-esteem)?
- What should Janis do now that she knows what her friend thinks about her?
- Is Emily a good friend?

4.2 Reframe It!

We need to challenge our negative thoughts and should always check out the evidence! Have a go at reframing the NATs in the table below. (The first one is done for you!)

How true might these thoughts be and how might you change the negative thoughts into more balanced ones?

NAT	REFRAME IT!
I can't do that sum!	That sum is difficult and I might find it hard, but I can ask for help.
I always get left out at break time!	
I never look as good as everyone else!	
My work is the worst!	
She gave me a dirty look because she doesn't like me!	
I'm stupid and thick!	
I won't get picked for the team!	
It's always my fault!	
I'll fail this test!	
He thinks I'm rubbish!	

4.3 My List of Positives

Sometimes we forget to think about the positive or good things that happen – this is not good! Every evening, think of at least one thing that has happened during the day that made you feel good. Record these on your positive scroll. At the end of the week look at the list – now you know that positive things really do happen to you!

4.4 Four Big NATs

Identify your four most common negative automatic thoughts. Then use the 'and so' strategy to think them through. Are these thoughts really logical?

Negative Thought 1	**Negative Thought 2**
And so, if this were true, what would this say about me? _____ _____	And so, if this were true, what would this say about me? _____ _____
And so, if this were true, what would this say about me? _____ _____	And so, if this were true, what would this say about me? _____ _____
Negative Thought 3	**Negative Thought 4**
And so, if this were true, what would this say about me? _____ _____	And so, if this were true, what would this say about me? _____ _____
And so, if this were true, what would this say about me? _____ _____	And so, if this were true, what would this say about me? _____ _____

Session 5

What Influences Us?

Introduction & Aims

In this session the focus is primarily on supporting the group to further recognise and manage their ineffective thinking patterns and processes. This is specifically related to the influences of key people in our lives and the ways in which bullying behaviours can lead to serious consequences. What we are ultimately trying to avoid are longer term mental health difficulties and the cycle of self-harming behaviours that can result for some of us when our ineffective thinking patterns become very entrenched.

The key aims are as follows:

- For the group to further consider what and who influences our thinking and to identify how we can know when this is a positive or negative thing.

- To understand and distinguish between the Six Errors of Ineffective Thinking and to begin to identify which errors we may be most prone to.

- To reflect upon how others may have made us feel bad or down and to specifically consider how we could have responded differently to two people in the past who have 'made' us feel less supported.

- For group members to gain a further understanding of bullying and to be clear about definitions and ways of bullying.

- To explore the group's perceptions regarding self-injury or self-harm and to distinguish between the myths and realities of such behaviours.

- To provide an opportunity for group members to reflect further on their own self-harming behaviours and the effects that these may be having on their overall well-being.

Warm-Up Activity

The aim of this activity is for the group members to begin to understand the differences between aggressive, passive and assertive behaviour. Choose from one of the following two activities:

1   In a circle each person says, 'Leave me alone,' in either an aggressive, passive or assertive way, and the other members of the group decide which of the three behaviours the person was displaying. It may be necessary for you to model all three types of behaviour.

2   Place three labels around the room: *aggressive, passive* and *assertive*. Now say various phrases in either an aggressive, passive or assertive manner. Group members have to stand by the label they think indicates which type of behaviour they think you were demonstrating. Phrases may include: 'Leave me alone,' 'I don't want to do that,' 'I don't think that will work for me,' and so on.

Icebreaker - A Question to Thought-Storm

The group can be asked to focus upon a key question in order to prompt thinking and awareness around some of the most important issues to be covered in this session. It will be essential to encourage everyone to participate and generate their own responses, but also to ensure that everyone feels safe in doing so. The responses can be recorded on a whiteboard or flip chart, as appropriate, and you can also highlight any similarities and differences in the responses. The idea is to begin to encourage a deeper level of thinking around the key issues via the process of cooperative idea-sharing.

The key question for this session is: What and who influences our thinking, and how do we know when this is a positive or negative thing?

Case Study 4 Questions for Discussion

Sam is feeling fed up as he feels under pressure to do drugs with his friends. They are saying that he is soft and that he should just go along with them as it is a laugh. He is getting more and more fed up, because they won't stop making comments. He is now beginning to believe them and think that perhaps they may be right and that he was probably just born to be boring (one of their comments). When they went to a friend's house last week, everyone there was smoking weed apart from him and the girl he really likes said he was just a kill joy. That really upset him and he's been feeling really down about it ever since. He doesn't know why he should feel so negative, but it just seems like their comments and hers are really starting to get to him. He has started to drink more and more – stealing the booze from his parents' drink cabinet – and this seems to be helping him blot it out.

- What kind of thoughts do you think Sam is having?
- What are the main pressures?
- How might his friends' comments be affecting him?
- Is he right about their opinions of him? Where is the evidence for this?
- If you were his friend, what advice would you give him?
- How can he break this cycle and how can he help himself?
- What should he be saying to his friends and thinking to himself?

Activities

5.1 Ineffective Thinking – the Six Errors

Explain to the group that the six most common thinking errors are as follows:

1 Doing down

2 Blowing up

3 Predicting failure

4 Over-emotional thoughts

5 Setting yourself up

6 Blaming yourself

Using Worksheet 5.1, discuss what each error involves and then give everyone some time to reflect and to consider whether they are guilty of engaging in any of these forms of ineffective thinking and how this might be affecting them in their daily lives. It may be helpful for the group to work in pairs or smaller groups and to share their experiences, highlighting any similarities and differences.

5.2 The Influence of Others

This activity reinforces the influence that others can have on our well-being and the development of our thinking habits and choices. Using Worksheet 5.2, ask the group members to consider the following questions:

- How have others influenced you?

- What did they do and say that made an impact upon you and the way that you think and feel about yourself?

Now ask everyone to think about two people who made them feel positive and what it was that these people said or did that had a positive influence.

Next, ask them to think about two people who did not make them feel supported and why this was.

In the whole group, consider why it really is so important for us as human beings to surround ourselves with positive rather than negative inputs and influences.

5.3 Bullying Information Sheet

When others make us feel down or we respond to them in a way which results in a low mood, it is important that we are able to distinguish between flippant nastiness and real bullying. Sometimes this line is not absolutely clear: someone may be in a bad mood themselves and simply be taking it out on us at this point in time.

Session 5   What Influences Us?

The information on Worksheet 5.3 is intended to provide some clarification, so ask the group to read it carefully before you discuss the contents. A clear definition is provided as follows:

Bullying is where someone hurts you either physically, by hitting or kicking you, or verbally by calling you names or teasing you.

Bullying can occur in a number of ways and these are also described on the worksheet. It is important to give the group adequate time to discuss these and to identify any issues that they might have in terms of recognising when a behaviour is bullying and when it is not.

5.4   Fact Versus Myth

Sometimes our ineffective thinking and personal problems and situations (including being bullied by peers, family, etc.) can be the root cause of self-harming behaviours, which are generally engaged in in order to manage the emotional pain and trauma.

The aim of this activity is to explore the group's perceptions regarding self-injury. Initiate a discussion by reading out some of the myths regarding self-harm from Worksheet 5.4. Before moving from one myth to the next, you should ensure that everyone understands the corresponding reality.

5.5   Identifying My Self-Harming Behaviours

In this final activity of the session the group are asked to consider how we all do things that may not be good for us. To some extent, we may all engage in some form of self-harming behaviours – including over-use of drugs, alcohol or engaging in ineffective thinking patterns.

Using Worksheet 5.5, ask everyone to try and list five things that they may do that may be harmful and to then give each one a rating of between 0 and 5, depending on how harmful they think it may be. Try to encourage further reflection and prompt the group to consider how they might reduce the most harmful behaviours in the future and what they might replace each of these with that could be more helpful to them in both the short and longer term.

Feedback & Reflections

Ask the group to reflect upon what they have learnt in the session, posing the following questions:

- What was useful for you in this session?
- What might have made the session more useful for you?
- What have you learnt about yourself in today's session?
- What have you learnt about others?
- How will you use your knowledge and skills to help yourself and others in the future?

The aim is to ensure that the group are able to reflect upon their knowledge and skills and also specifically to identify how and when they might transfer these into new situations in the future.

5.1 Ineffective Thinking - the Six Errors

1 DOING DOWN	2 BLOWING UP
▪ Only focusing on negatives. ▪ Only seeing the bad bit in something that was good overall. ▪ Not counting a positive, for example: 'He only wants to go out with me because he can't find anyone else.'	▪ Making things worse than they are. ▪ It's all or nothing, for example: 'I only got 78% and not 100% – it's not good enough!' ▪ Magnifying the problem, for example: 'I got the answer wrong and everyone in the class laughed at me! It's a catastrophe! I'll never get over it!'
3 PREDICTING FAILURE	**4 OVER-EMOTIONAL THOUGHTS**
▪ Mind-reading to predict failure, for example: 'I bet they are all laughing at me! I know he hates me!' ▪ Fortune-telling – knowing you will fail, for example: 'I know I won't be able to do that work,' or 'I know they won't like me.'	▪ With this Faulty Thinking our emotions become very strong and cloud the way we think and understand things. ▪ Because we feel bad, we presume everything *is* bad – the emotions take over! ▪ We attach negative labels to ourselves, for example: 'I'm rubbish/stupid/a loser ...'
5 SETTING YOURSELF UP	**6 BLAMING YOURSELF**
▪ Setting targets too high and setting ourselves up to fail. ▪ '*I should*', '*I must*', '*I can't*', '*I want*', '*I shouldn't*', and so on. ▪ Creating an impossible standard to achieve.	▪ Everything that goes wrong or is wrong is our fault – even stuff we have no control over! For example: 'I got into my car and it broke down!' Or, 'I turned on the computer and it crashed!'

5.2 The Influence of Others

Other people can have both negative and positive influences on our well-being and the development of our thinking habits and choices.

How have others influenced you?

What did they do and say that made an impact upon you and the way that you think and feel about yourself?

1   Think about two people who have influenced you in a positive way, and write down the helpful things that they said and did in order to make you feel positive about yourself.

	PERSON 1	**PERSON 2**
They said	_____	_____
	_____	_____
	_____	_____
	_____	_____
They did	_____	_____
	_____	_____
	_____	_____
	_____	_____

2   Now identify two people who did not make you feel supported and think about what they said and did.

	PERSON 1	**PERSON 2**
They said	_____	_____
	_____	_____
	_____	_____
	_____	_____
They did	_____	_____
	_____	_____
	_____	_____
	_____	_____

STOP & REFLECT

◼ Could you have responded differently to the two people who 'made' you feel less supported?

◼ How might you have responded differently?

◼ Discuss this with a partner.

5.3 Bullying Information Sheet

Bullying is when someone hurts you either physically (by hitting or kicking you), or verbally (by calling you names or teasing you).

Bullying can happen in a number of ways. Someone might be bullying you if they are:

- calling you names
- spreading lies about you
- teasing you
- hitting or kicking you and causing you physical pain
- pushing or pulling you about
- taking your money or possessions
- leaving you out or excluding you
- threatening or intimidating you
- texting you horrible messages
- filming you on their mobile phones and spreading it about
- sending you horrible emails or messages on Facebook and other social networking websites.

There are other types of more specific bullying:

Homophobic bullying

Somebody may bully you if you are of a different sexual orientation to them: for example, someone straight might bully you if you are gay and call you 'gay' as an insult.

Racist bullying

People may bully you because of the colour of your skin, and so would call you horrible names linked to your skin colour.

Size-ist bullying

Someone may bully you because of your size, calling you 'fat' or 'skinny' as an insult.

Sexist bullying

People bully you for being the opposite sex, calling you 'weak' if you are a girl, for example.

Page 1 of 2

People may also bully you if you are different from them, if you look different and have a different colour of hair, or wear glasses. People sometimes bully other people because of from where they come from or their social class, so they may call you a 'chav' or a 'snob'. People also bully other people if they are not as intelligent as them – or if they are more intelligent than them.

Anyone can be bullied. Sometimes people pick on something that makes you different from everyone else or if you wear different clothes. Sometimes there is no particular reason at all for someone to bully you. Sometimes the bullying is a one-off. Other times, someone can bully someone else for a long period of time.

Around 70 per cent of young people have been bullied at one time and one million children are bullied every week.

Bullying can upset you, hurt you, make you feel isolated and worthless, lonely, lacking in confidence, anxious and angry. Being bullied can affect your mental health. People who are being bullied can develop other problems such as depression, anxiety and eating problems and may self-harm or turn to drugs and alcohol.

Bullying in any form is hurtful and unacceptable.

If you are being bullied, you need to talk to someone and get help.

Page 2 of 2

5.4 Fact Versus Myth

People have many different thoughts about self-harm or self-injury. The table below shows some of the more common myths about self-harm and also what the realities are.

The Myth	The Reality
People who self-harm are attention-seeking.	If attention is the reason for self-harming, there are far less painful and degrading ways of getting it.
People who self-harm are manipulative.	Self-harm is usually carried out in private. Much of the self-harming that occurs goes undiscovered. Many of those who self-harm go to great lengths to make sure it goes undiscovered.
Self-harmers need to see a psychiatrist in order to get better.	Psychiatry alone has had little success helping those who self-harm.
People who self-harm tend to be teenage girls and they grow out of it.	Recent research shows that there is less difference in the rates of self-injury between men and women than previously thought and there is no evidence that people 'grow out of it'.

5.5 Identifying My Self-Harming Behaviours

We all do things that may not be good for us. Try and list five things you do which may be harmful. Give each one a rating of between 0 and 5, according to how harmful you think it may be.

What I do	Rating
1	0 1 2 3 4 5 Not harmful at all – very harmful
2	0 1 2 3 4 5 Not harmful at all – very harmful
3	0 1 2 3 4 5 Not harmful at all – very harmful
4	0 1 2 3 4 5 Not harmful at all – very harmful
5	0 1 2 3 4 5 Not harmful at all – very harmful

List the things you do which you would like to change and those you would like to continue. Give a reason for each one.

▨ I would like to stop doing the following:

Activity	**Reason**
_____	_____
_____	_____
_____	_____
_____	_____
_____	_____

▨ I will carry on doing the following:

Activity	**Reason**
_____	_____
_____	_____
_____	_____
_____	_____

Session 6

Core Beliefs & Making the Connections

Introduction & Aims

In this session the focus is primarily on supporting the group to further recognise and manage their ineffective thinking patterns and processes. This is specifically related to the influences of key people in our lives. It is vital to know where our beliefs about ourselves come from and know that we can and should change these if they make us feel bad and useless.

The key aims are as follows:

- For group members to further understand where our beliefs about ourselves come from and how we can change these if they make us feel bad and useless.

- To identify the most significant core belief that each group member has and to challenge this effectively.

- For group members to further develop their skills in recognising the antecedents to negative beliefs, thoughts and feelings and to see these links and further recognise the pitfalls.

- To recognise the positive circles of influence in our lives and to understand the need to reduce or eliminate those that are not helpful to us or possibly damaging to our well-being and mindset.

- To further understand that changing our thinking takes time and effort and that we get better at this with practice and that using self-monitoring tools and strategies can help us in this process.

Warm-Up Activity

The aim of the warm-up activity is for the group members to begin to identify characteristics that they consider are important in their friends. In pairs, ask everyone to identify the two most important qualities that they think make a good friend. For example: you can have a laugh with them; they can be trusted to keep things secret; they are there for you. Each person then provides feedback on one of the qualities in a whole group discussion.

Session 6 Core Beliefs & Making the Connections

Icebreaker - A Question to Thought-Storm

The group can be asked to focus upon a key question in order to prompt thinking and awareness around some of the most important issues to be covered in this session. It will be essential to encourage everyone to participate and generate their own responses, but also to ensure that everyone feels safe in doing so. The responses can be recorded on a whiteboard or flip chart, as appropriate, and you can also highlight any similarities and differences in the responses. The idea is to begin to encourage a deeper level of thinking around the key issues via the process of cooperative idea-sharing.

The key question for this session is: Where do our beliefs about ourselves come from and can we change these if they make us feel bad and useless?

Case Study & Questions for Discussion

Meera has known for some time that one of her core beliefs is that you have to be a true and loyal friend, and that this means being kind and generous to your friends. She goes around with a group of girls who have similar interests – all are into make-up and clothes and want to look their best. Some of them want to be models. The problem is that the clothes and make-up are all quite expensive and some of her friends don't have as much money as her, so she has started to sub them. She is now giving them all of her allowance, but they keep on saying that they need more, which is making it really difficult for her. She feels bad, because last week she took £50 from her father's wallet so she could help Amy buy a new top. The problem is that if she doesn't do this, she feels she will lose her friends – and rightly so, as she is richer than they are and being a good friend means that she should really help them out in this way.

- What kind of thoughts do you think Meera is having?
- What are the thinking errors she is making?
- What are the main pressures she is feeling?
- How might her core belief be unhelpful now?
- Is she right to think that her friends are 'real' friends?
- If you were her friend, what advice would you give her?
- How can she break this cycle and what should she do now to help herself?

Activities

6.1 More on Core Beliefs - the Challenge!

In this activity the group members are asked to focus on one specific, key and central core belief that they hold, making use of Worksheet 6.1. This builds on the previous core belief activity. As this is a key skill, it is very important that the group really do master this approach to identifying the advantages and disadvantages of holding core beliefs that may well not be helpful to them – either in the short or long term.

6.2   Making the Connections

Explain that this activity helps to reinforce the idea of the links between specific situations and the beliefs, thoughts, feelings and actions that they then generate. Ask the group to place themselves in the shoes of another by considering the responses people might have in a range of situations and completing the ideas they have on Worksheet 6.2. Make sure you leave time at the end of the activity for feedback and sharing of responses, so that everyone can consider how their ideas and responses may differ or be similar to those of the others in the group.

6.3   Positive Circles of Acceptance – Beat the Vampires!

Ask everyone to complete the Positive Circles of Acceptance on Worksheet 6.3 by writing in names of all the people they know who make them feel accepted. Then ask them to identify three people from the chart and to think about and record what these people think, say and do in order to make them feel accepted. For the second part of the activity they need to identify three people who do the opposite to this and record what they think, say and do. They can then reflect on this response and answer the following questions: Do you need these people if this is how they respond to you? How can you beat 'the vampires'?

Once again, the focus is on reinforcing the importance of recognising those people and situations in our lives which are draining, negative and ultimately unhealthy and ensuring that we can and do eliminate these from our thinking and interactions as far as possible. In this way, we will be helping ourselves to maintain well-being and a more positive mindset.

6.4   Changing our Thinking – Sustain the Change by Recording It!

Worksheet 6.4 provides the group members with another key strategy or technique for sustaining positive thinking in order to ensure continued behavioural change. Ask everyone to identify a core belief that they need to challenge and change and to then commit to making that key change in thinking by reframing the NAT that results from holding onto this belief. The worksheet serves as a diary for them to record their reframes and the outcomes throughout the following week.

Feedback & Reflections

Ask the group to reflect upon what they have learnt in the session, posing the following questions:

- What was useful for you in this session?
- What might have made the session more useful for you?
- What have you learnt about yourself in today's session?
- What have you learnt about others?
- How will you use your knowledge and skills to help yourself and others in the future?

The aim is to ensure that the group are able to reflect upon their knowledge and skills and also specifically to identify how and when they might transfer these into new situations in the future.

6.1 More on Core Beliefs - the Challenge!

Think about your one main core belief and write it below. Then focus on the advantages and disadvantages to holding this belief.

My Core Belief _____

_____

Advantages of holding this belief	Disadvantages of holding this belief

6.2 Making the Connections

Our core beliefs and thoughts can affect our emotions and behaviour in certain situations. How we interpret events and make sense of them can lead us to respond in negative or positive ways. It is important that we have the self-knowledge and ability to reflect on our responses and see the link between our reactions and the consequences of our behaviours.

In the table below the first situation is completed, showing the important beliefs or thoughts that were triggered by the situation and the emotions/consequences of those beliefs or thoughts. What do you think the beliefs and thoughts (or their emotional consequences) might be in the other situations?

Antecedent or Situation A	Beliefs & Thoughts B	Consequences: Emotions & Behaviours C
Your friend doesn't ring when she says she will.	How inconvenient! I can't go out until she's phoned.	Angry
Your sister is upset, claiming she has no friends.		Guilty
Your dad forgets to buy you a birthday present.	I always remember his birthday, so why didn't he remember mine? It's not fair.	
You make a mistake in front of your form group.		Highly anxious
You seek therapy for panic attacks.		Ashamed
You didn't get the part in the school play you wanted.		Depressed
Your friend has a succession of attractive boyfriends/girlfriends.	They only go out with my friend because she/he is rich. If my friend lost it all, they'd be dumped.	

Page 1 of 2

Antecedent or Situation A	Beliefs & Thoughts B	Consequences: Emotions & Behaviours C
You are stuck in a traffic jam and will be late for school.		Angry
You are stuck in a traffic jam and will be late for school.		Calm
You are feeling hot and sweaty in a crowded lift.	I can't get my breath. There's no air. I'm going to suffocate.	
Your current relationship ends.		Happy
You blush in a group.		Embarrassed
Your boyfriend/girlfriend dances with someone else at a party.	He/she probably fancies this other person. They are very good looking. What's wrong with my company?	
Your teacher does not reply when you say 'good morning' to her.		Worried
Your teacher does not reply when you say 'good morning' to her.		Unconcerned
You are going to be late for an important exam.	My teachers will think I'm undisciplined and unprofessional. I won't be taken seriously. I'll lose their respect.	
You are blamed for something you did not do	It wasn't my fault. I would never do anything like that. Why have they picked on me? I don't deserve this.	
You fail an exam.		Depressed

Page 2 of 2

6.3 Positive Circles of Acceptance - Beat the Vampires!

Complete the positive Circles of Acceptance by writing in the names of all the people you know who make you feel accepted.

Identify three people from your circle. Record what they think, say and do in order to make you feel accepted:

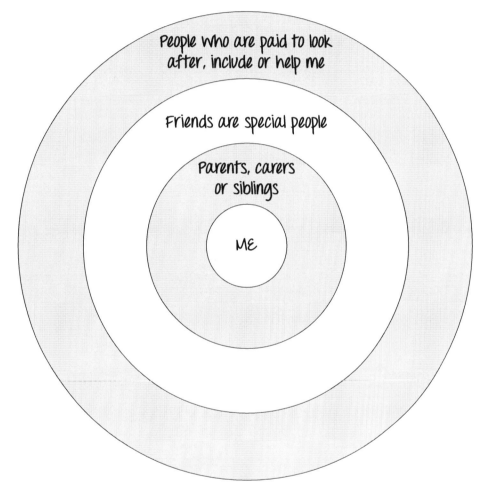

Person 1 thinks _____

says _____

does _____

Person 2 thinks _____

says _____

does _____

Person 3 thinks _____

says _____

does _____

Page 1 of 2

Next identify 3 people who do the opposite to this and record what they think, say and do. Reflect on this response to you.

Person 1   thinks _____

_____

says _____

_____

does _____

_____

Person 2   thinks _____

_____

says _____

_____

does _____

_____

Person 3   thinks _____

_____

says _____

_____

does _____

_____

■   Do you need these people if this is how they respond to you?

■   How can you beat 'the vampires'?

Page 2 of 2

6.4 Changing our Thinking - Sustain the Change by Recording It!

The core belief that I need to challenge and change is:

_____

_____

I will do this by reframing the NAT that results from holding onto this belief and keep a dairy for one week recording my reframes and the outcomes.

The trigger to my NAT	How I felt	How I reframed this	How did this help?	What was the outcome?
Sunday				
Monday				
Tuesday				
Wednesday				
Thursday				
Friday				
Saturday				

Beat the Blues

Introduction & Aims

In this session the focus is primarily on supporting the group members to recognise and understand that stress is a normal part of our lives, but that we can also be proactive in managing this and in specifically 'beating the blues'. Being able to engage in reliable self-help strategies when we feel low is very important for our well-being overall. These are life skills that will ultimately help to protect us from more serious mental health difficulties and problems in the future.

The key aims are as follows:

- For group members to be able to identify and articulate their own personal strategies for managing uncomfortable feelings and a low mood.

- To be able to identify the most healthy options and least healthy options in terms of maintaining positive mental and physical health.

- For group members to begin to understand the link between happiness and the showing of gratitude, and to recognise the fact that people who are grateful tend to be happier, healthier and more fulfilled. They can also understand that being grateful can help people cope with stress and can even have a beneficial effect on heart rate.

- To similarly understand that doing things for others has a positive impact on our well-being; to maintain a log of such acts of kindness and to reflect upon the outcomes.

- For group members to be introduced to the five happy habits from the positive psychology approach, as well as to realise that we can all engage in and understand how these can increase our positive feelings and sense of well-being.

Warm-Up Activity

This warm-up activity is entitled 'The Frozen Lake'. The group are asked to imagine that they are on a frozen lake. They are then asked to act out how they would move around the lake and identify what they'd say and feel in such a situation.

You can join in this activity with the group. It can be further developed in the following ways:

- Imagine you are in a pit full of snakes.

- Imagine you are in a vat full of jelly.

- Imagine you are in a deep, dark box, … and so on.

The activity encourages the group members to express themselves both verbally and non-verbally and to identify the range of often strong feelings that they may experience in each situation.

Icebreaker – A Question to Thought-Storm

The group can be asked to focus upon a key question in order to prompt thinking and awareness around some of the most important issues to be covered in this session. It will be essential to encourage everyone to participate and generate their own responses, but also to ensure that everyone feels safe in doing so. The responses can be recorded on a whiteboard or flip chart, as appropriate, and you can also highlight any similarities and differences in the responses. The idea is to begin to encourage a deeper level of thinking around the key issues via the process of cooperative idea-sharing.

The key question for this session is: What strategies do you use to help yourself beat the blues? What works for us and why?

Case Study & Questions for Discussion

Hazel is getting anxious as she has to start a new school next term when her family move down to Devon from London. She is really worried about making this transition as she knows that she is shy and finds it really difficult to make friends. She has two good friends at her current school, but those relationships took a long time to build, mainly because she found it so difficult to trust people and to accept that they would like her for who she is. She was bullied at primary school, so finds it very difficult to trust other girls. Recently, she has been experiencing a real sense of dread and feels sick in her stomach even at the thought of her change of school. She has tried to talk to her brother about this, but he has just split up with his girlfriend so he's not really interested.

- What kind of thoughts do you think Hazel is having?

- What are the main pressures she is experiencing?

- How might her previous experience of being bullied be feeding into this?

- Is she right to anticipate that this will happen again in her new school? Where is the evidence for this?

- If you were her friend, what advice would you give her?

- How can she break this cycle and where can she get the best help?

Activities

7.1 Mental & Physical Fitness Ideas

Give everyone a copy of Worksheet 7.1 and ask them to cut out the statements that illustrate healthy and unhealthy options in terms of mental and physical fitness. Ask them to sort them into order, according to the most healthy and least healthy options for maintaining positive mental and physical health. Ask the group to discuss their choices both in pairs and then in the whole group to share ideas and identify similarities and differences in their responses.

7.2 A Gratitude Journal – Three Good Things

Start a discussion among the group about how being grateful is about much more than just saying thank you – it's about not taking things for granted and having a sense of appreciation and thankfulness for life. People who are grateful tend to be happier, healthier and more fulfilled. Being grateful can help people cope with stress and can even have a beneficial effect on heart rate. For this reason, you are going to ask the group to keep a gratitude diary for one week. Each day they need to write down three good things that have happened to them or others in their lives. These events can be anything they feel good about or grateful for.

It is important to emphasise that even on a bad day there are normally some things that we can feel good about, however small. Taking time to be grateful is not about ignoring the bad things – it just helps us focus our attention more on the positive, rather than dwell on the negative.

In order to get used to the idea, the group can start by filling in the boxes on Worksheet 7.2 in order to describe three good things that happened to them yesterday and why they were good. The aim is to raise awareness and thinking around such activities and reinforce the value of appreciating the good things in our lives and the benefit this has in maintaining overall well-being.

7.3 Do Something for Others! Keep a Kindness Diary

Explain to the group that you are going to ask them to engage in positive acts that generate positive feelings and thoughts. They should try to do something good and kind for others at least once a day, each day for a week.

They can use Worksheet 7.3 to record their acts of kindness. Encourage everyone to note down how they felt about doing these acts and whether they found them easy or difficult to complete.

The aim of this activity is to enable the group to reflect upon how good they feel when they are not just thinking of themselves.

7.4 Happy Habits

Worksheet 7.4 lists five things we can all do to make ourselves happier. Ask everyone to look at each one in turn and then, for each, think about and formulate a personal target and strategy for reaching that target.

Feedback & Reflections

Ask the group to reflect upon what they have learnt in the session, posing the following questions:

- What was useful for you in this session?
- What might have made the session more useful for you?
- What have you learnt about yourself in today's session?
- What have you learnt about others?
- How will you use your knowledge and skills to help yourself and others in the future?

The aim is to ensure that the group are able to reflect upon their knowledge and skills and also specifically to identify how and when they might transfer these into new situations in the future.

7.1 Mental & Physical Fitness Ideas

Cut out these statements and then sort them into order according to the most healthy and least healthy options for maintaining positive mental and physical health.

Taking regular exercise	Not eating junk food
Going to lots of parties	Having unprotected sex
Sleeping for 7 to 9 hours a night	Feeling happy
Having low self-esteem	Feeling confident
Using stress busters	Enjoying hobbies
Eating fruit and vegetables	Reframing those NATS
Not smoking or taking drugs	Liking other people and doing things for them
Eating a low fat diet	Being optimistic
Not eating sweets or too much sugar	Eating at regular times
Having good friends	Doing acts of kindness
Eating fibre each day	Being able to relax
Drinking a lot of alcohol	A high fat diet
Being the 'right' weight for your height	Not getting anxious about things

Compare your sequence with a partner. Do you agree on what constitutes a healthy lifestyle that promotes and maintains well-being? Can you justify your ideas?

7.2 A Gratitude Journal - Three Good Things

Being grateful is about much more than just saying thank you – it's about not taking things for granted and having a sense of appreciation and thankfulness for life.

People who are grateful tend to be happier, healthier and more fulfilled. Being grateful can help people cope with stress and can even have a beneficial effect on heart rate.

Each day write down three good things that have happened. They can be anything you feel good about or grateful for.

Even on a bad day there are normally some things that we can feel good about. Taking time to be grateful is not about ignoring the bad things – it just helps us focus our attention more on the positive, rather than dwell on the negative.

To get used to the idea, start by filling in the boxes below to describe three good things that happened to you **yesterday** and why they were good.

Try to include **why** you felt each of the things was really good.

Good Thing 1
Good Thing 2
Good Thing 3

Now repeat this activity **at the end of each day** for a week. Keep a Gratitude Journal and write down your 'Three Good Things' each day.

7.3 Do Something for Others! Keep a Kindness Diary

Do something good and kind for others at least once a day, each day for a week.

Use this sheet to keep a record of your acts of kindness. You can also note down how you felt about doing them and whether you found them easy or difficult. Take time to think how good you feel when you are not just thinking of yourself!

1 Day/date:
What did you do? Who for? How did it go?

2 Day/date:
What did you do? Who for? How did it go?

3 Day/date:
What did you do? Who for? How did it go?

4 Day/date:
What did you do? Who for? How did it go?

5 Day/date:
What did you do? Who for? How did it go?

6 Day/date:
What did you do? Who for? How did it go?

7 Day/date:
What did you do? Who for? How did it go?

7.4 Happy Habits

There are five things we can do to make ourselves happier. Look at each habit and then think about and come up with a personal target and a strategy for reaching this for each one.

	My target	My strategy
1 Make lots of friends and be kind to them.		
2 Be grateful for what you have every day.		
3 Don't compare yourself badly with others.		
4 Don't compare yourself to those in the media/ famous personalities.		
5 Savour your experiences.		

Introduction & Aims

In this session the focus is primarily on supporting the group to recognise and understand that change is a normal part of our lives, but that we can also be proactive in managing this – specifically in 'recognising ambivalence and planning for and accepting relapse.' Being able to understand how change works as a process can ultimately help us to maintain well-being and keep things in better perspective when they may appear to be going wrong. These are more of the essential life skills that will ultimately help to protect us from falling back into ineffective thinking patterns in the future.

The key aims are as follows:

- For the group members to begin to consider if and how we change ourselves for the better and to understand that our past does not have to dictate our future.

- To understand and work through the stages that we go through when we are trying to make a change in our behaviour, thoughts, feelings or habits, as follows: **Contemplation** – when we think about making a change; **Preparation** – when we prepare to make the change and identify what can help us in the process; **Action** – when we make the change; **Maintenance** – when we try to keep it going and don't revert back to old habits; and **Relapse** – when we fail and get it wrong again before thinking about trying again.

- For the group members to all have the opportunity to think through the stages for their problem/issue; for each person to identify a change that they made in the past and try to record what they thought and said to themselves at each stage.

- To understand the importance of making a plan for when we relapse and to think through a stepped approach to planning for such eventualities.

- For group members to be able to begin to set realistic goals, breaking the steps down into smaller ones if they don't succeed initially.

Warm-up Activity

The aim of this activity is to gently introduce the topic of fear in terms of us fearing the notion or concept of change. Prepare a set of picture cards reflecting objects or experiences that often elicit fear – these can easily be found online. The picture cards should be copied in advance, laminated and placed in a non-transparent wallet or envelope. Blank cards should be included to give each person an opportunity to generate their own ideas. Begin by removing a picture

Session 8   The Change Cycle

card from the wallet, naming the object or situation, and placing the card, face-up, on the floor in the centre of the circle. Each group member then takes a turn to remove a card, name it and place it randomly in the middle of the circle.

When everyone has had a turn and all the picture cards are on the floor, place the blank cards on the floor and encourage a discussion by asking:

- What do you notice about these cards?
- What do you think the cards have in common?
- What would you put on the blank cards?

Icebreaker – A Question to Thought-Storm

The group can be asked to focus upon a key question in order to prompt thinking and awareness around some of the most important issues to be covered in this session. It will be essential to encourage everyone to participate and generate their own responses, but also to ensure that everyone feels safe in doing so. The responses can be recorded on a whiteboard or flip chart, as appropriate, and you can also highlight any similarities and differences in the responses. The idea is to begin to encourage a deeper level of thinking around the key issues via the process of cooperative idea-sharing.

The key question for this session is: Can we change ourselves for the better or does our past have to dictate our future?

Case Study & Questions for Discussion

Marcus has been smoking now for two years. He has managed to hide this from his mum as she's a smoker too, so she probably doesn't notice the smell so much and she also works very long hours; she often doesn't get in from work until well after he has gone to his room. The problem is now that he has been picked for the trials for the QPR junior team and knows that this is his big chance. However, he is beginning to get really worried about his level of fitness, because he is finding that his running isn't quite as good as it was: he is getting slightly slower, which he now feels might well be a big issue. He really wants to get his smoking under control. If he's really honest he wants to stop altogether, but he just can't. He gives up for a few days and then gets a real craving and just gives into it again. He thinks he's just got no willpower and is basically a weak person and this is getting him down, because he knows that weak people just don't get into top class teams – and that's his ultimate dream.

- What kind of thoughts do you think Marcus is having?
- What are the main pressures for him at the moment?
- How might the prospect of the QPR trials be affecting him?
- Is he right about not ever being able to stop smoking? Where is the evidence for this?
- Is he right to think that he is 'weak'? What is the evidence for this?

- Do people have to fail before they succeed?

- If you were his friend, what advice would you give him?

- How can he break this cycle and where can he get the best help?

Activities

8.1 The Change Cycle

This activity introduces everyone to the Change Cycle and Worksheet 8.1 provides them with a visual image of the stages of change. The simple diagram illustrates the stages of change that we go through when we are trying to make a change in our behaviour, thoughts, feelings or habits. We will go through the following stages:

1 **Contemplation** – when we think about making a change.

2 **Preparation** – when we prepare to make the change and identify what can help us in the process.

3 **Action** – when we make the change.

4 **Maintenance** – when we try to keep it going and don't revert back to old habits.

5 **Relapse** – when we fail and get it wrong, before thinking about trying again!

Discuss among the group these different stages and then ask them to think about a change that they have tried to make in the past.

Form pairs and then discuss this with a partner, focusing on the following questions:

- Do you think that you went through these stages?

- Did you relapse and how did this feel?

- If relapse is a 'normal' part of the process, what does this tell you?

- Should we expect to fail at some points and is this okay, as long as we learn from such relapses?

Everyone can then feedback their main discussion points to the group as a whole.

8.2 Thinking Through the Stages for My Problem or Issue

Ask everyone to identify a change that they have made in the past and, using Worksheet 8.2, try to record what they thought and said to themselves at each stage of the process. This will help to reinforce their understanding of the stages of change and the narratives that they may construct at each stage as they progress through the cycle.

8.3 Coping with Relapse & Making the Plan

Discuss with the whole group how when we relapse and revert back to an old behaviour after trying hard to change it we can feel angry or sad and experience some difficult emotions and questions. Why did I let myself down? Why did this go wrong? Why couldn't I be successful? We can have a tendency to blame ourselves or others for this, to get caught up in a negative cycle of thinking and behaviour, and to fall into the self-fulfilling prophecy trap.

This activity explains that what we should do is make a plan for when we relapse, as this is likely to happen. Encourage everyone to work through the stepped approach on Worksheet 8.3 in order to plan for such a relapse.

8.4 Focus on the Problem

Worksheet 8.4 provides a framework for further analysing and reflecting upon problems that group members might wish to change. Ask the group to use the worksheet and to work through each stage of the process in turn. Once completed, ask the group to form pairs and discuss the process and the outcomes with their partner.

8.5 My Goals

Using Worksheet 8.5, group members can work through a framework for identifying realistic goals that are truly authentic. They can ponder on specific areas or questions as follows: Am I ready to change? What is the change that I may want and need to make? Can I visualise myself making the change? Discuss the ideas for reaching goals in pairs and then with the whole group.

Feedback & Reflections

Ask the group to reflect upon what they have learnt in the session, posing the following questions:

- What was useful for you in this session?
- What might have made the session more useful for you?
- What have you learnt about yourself in today's session?
- What have you learnt about others?
- How will you use your knowledge and skills to help yourself and others in the future?

The aim is to ensure that the group are able to reflect upon their knowledge and skills and also specifically to identify how and when they might transfer these into new situations in the future.

8.1 The Change Cycle

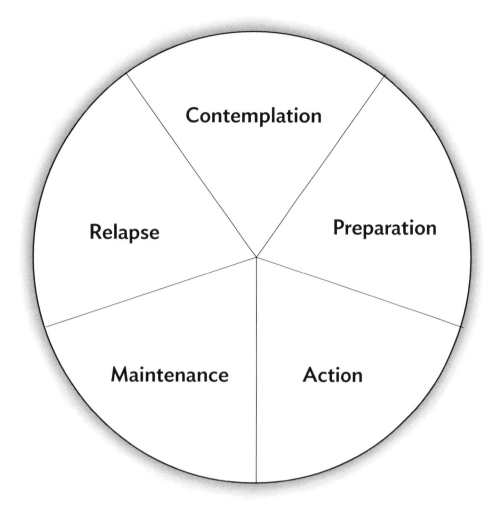

This diagram illustrates the stages of change that we go through when we are trying to make a change in our behaviour, thoughts, feelings or habits. We will go through the following stages:

1 **Contemplation** – when we think about making a change.

2 **Preparation** – when we prepare to make the change and identify what can help us in the process.

3 **Action** – when we make the change.

4 **Maintenance** – when we try to keep it going and don't revert back to old habits.

5 **Relapse** – when we fail and get it wrong before thinking about trying again!

Think about a change that you have tried to make in the past and discuss this with a partner.

 ■ Do you think that you went through these stages?

 ■ Did you relapse and how did this feel?

If relapse is a 'normal' part of the process, what does this tell you? Should we expect to fail at some points and is this OK, as long as we learn from such relapses?

Feedback your main discussion points to the group.

8.2 Thinking Through the Stages for My Problem or Issue

Think about a change that you have made in the past and try to record what you thought and said to yourself at each stage.

The change I tried to make was: _____

This is what I said or thought at each stage:

1   **Contemplation** – when I thought about making a change.

_____

_____

_____

2   **Preparation** – when I prepared to make the change and identified what could help me in the process.

_____

_____

_____

3   **Action** – when I made the change.

_____

_____

_____

4   **Maintenance** – when I tried to keep it going and didn't revert back to old habits.

_____

_____

_____

5   **Relapse** –   when I failed and got it wrong, before thinking about trying again!

_____

_____

_____

_____

8.3 Coping with Relapse & Making the Plan

When we relapse and revert back to an old behaviour after trying hard to change it, we can feel angry or sad and experience some difficult emotions and questions. Why did I let myself down? Why did this go wrong? Why couldn't I be successful? We can have a tendency to blame ourselves or others for this, to get caught up in a negative cycle of thinking and behaviour, and to fall into the self-fulfilling prophecy trap.

What we *should* do is make a plan for when we relapse! Work through the stepped approach as follows:

Identify the change that you would like to make now:

_____

If you relapse, identify the following:

■ Who will help me to talk it through and give me the best support, advice and encouragement?

_____

■ What three practical steps can I take to think about and plan to try again?

_____

_____

_____

■ How are these steps better or more appropriate than the ones I took last time?

_____

_____

■ What I will do: first, second and third.

_____

_____

_____

■ What 'self-talk' or script can I develop to feel positive again about trying once more?

_____

_____

■ My 'self-talk' script will be as follows: _____

_____

_____

_____

8.4 Focus on the Problem

This activity gives you a helpful framework for analysing and reflecting on a problem you want to change.

What is your problem? _____

_____

_____

_____

_____

_____

_____

1 How serious is it on a scale of 0 to 10, where 10 is the most serious problem?

Comments: _____

_____

_____

_____

2 How serious do your teachers think it is, on the scale of 0 to 10?

Comments: _____

_____

_____

_____

Page 1 of 2

3 How serious do your parents or carers think it is, on the scale of 0 to 10?

Comments: _____

_____

_____

_____

4 How do you prefer to deal with this problem?

_____

_____

_____

_____

5 How helpful do you think it would be to talk to someone about this problem on the scale of 0 to 10, where 10 is 'very helpful'?

6 What would change if this problem gets better?

_____

_____

_____

_____

7 To what degree would you be prepared to change something about yourself to make things better? Use the 0 to 10 scale to rate how prepared you are, where 10 is 'very prepared'.

Comments: _____

_____

_____

_____

_____

Page 2 of 2

8.5 My Goals

This activity will help you to identify two realistic goals and to find ways to achieve these.

My first goal _____

Are you ready to change?

Not ready   0   1   2   3   4   5   6   7   8   9   10   Ready

How important is this goal to you / your parents / your teacher?

Not important   0   1   2   3   4   5   6   7   8   9   10   Important

How confident are you that you can change?

Not confident   0   1   2   3   4   5   6   7   8   9   10   Very confident

How do you rate yourself now?

0   1   2   3   4   5   6   7   8   9   10

How much do you (realistically) expect to change?

0   1   2   3   4   5   6   7   8   9   10

My second goal _____

Are you ready to change?

Not ready   0   1   2   3   4   5   6   7   8   9   10   Ready

How important is this goal to you / your parents / your teacher?

Not important   0   1   2   3   4   5   6   7   8   9   10   Important

How confident are you that you can change?

Not confident   0   1   2   3   4   5   6   7   8   9   10   Very confident

How do you rate yourself now?

0   1   2   3   4   5   6   7   8   9   10

How much do you (realistically) expect to change?

0   1   2   3   4   5   6   7   8   9   10

Page 1 of 2

My main challenge:

Stage 1 – My steps to succeed are:

1

2

3

Stage 2 – My coping self-talk is:

Stage 3 – Visualise Yourself being Successful

Repeat your coping self-talk while you imagine reaching your first step! Keep practising this.

Stage 4 – Experiment!

Pick a time to face your fear or challenge – TRY IT OUT – take your first step and use your self-talk

Stage 5 – Reward!

Treat yourself for being successful.

Don't give up! Keep going!

Break the steps down into smaller ones if you don't succeed at first.

Page 2 of 2

Session 9

How to See Failure

Introduction & Aims

In this session the focus is primarily on supporting the group to recognise and understand that making mistakes is a normal part of our lives, but that we can also be proactive in learning from them and in developing our skills and strategies for 'bouncing back'. Developing our resilience and learning from the things that we got wrong are key essentials in terms of maintaining effective thinking and behaviours, both in the short and longer term. We need to learn how to focus more on the solutions to a problem, to recognise even the smallest changes and successes, and to set ourselves appropriate and realistic goals.

The key aims are as follows:

- For the group members to discuss and consider the notion that the only bad mistake is the one we don't learn from and to begin to move away from ineffective thinking that would suggest otherwise.

- To engage in the process of problem definition and using exceptions, as well as beginning to understand why this way of reflecting on a problem is more constructive and positive than simply presenting the problem.

- To understand the concept of a 'good' failure, by identifying a personal failure and then considering what has been learnt from this and how we might respond more positively and effectively next time we encountered the same or a similar situation.

- For group members to begin to understand the concept of resilience and the fact that we all need to be able to 'bounce back' after we have experienced a setback. Group members are given the opportunity to recognise and articulate ways in which they have been able to bounce back and the skills and personal qualities they have used to do this.

- For group members to learn the importance and usefulness of focusing on the solutions to a problem, as opposed to the problem itself.

Warm-up Activity

This activity is called 'The Shopping List'. People often value material things and can be envious of what their friends have. The aim is to encourage the group to start thinking about material things and their value in a fun way.

Ask everyone to form a circle, then start the activity by saying, 'I went shopping and I bought …' This sentence then gets passed around the whole circle, so that each person adds an item to the shopping list.

The game can either be played so that each person adds their own item only, or lists the previous items before adding their own item. Further rounds can be played adding the amounts spent (for example, 'I went shopping and I bought a pair of jeans for £100), or focusing on particular categories of item (for example, stationery, clothes, cars, and so on).

When three or four rounds have been played (depending on group size and the group's response) encourage a group discussion by asking the following questions:

- Did you notice anything about the items on our shopping list?
- Do you think one person could own all these items?
- Do you think one person would need all these items?
- Can you make a connection between this activity and the topic for today?

Icebreaker - A Question to Thought-Storm

The group can be asked to focus upon a key question in order to prompt thinking and awareness around some of the most important issues to be covered in this session. It will be essential to encourage everyone to participate and generate their own responses, but also to ensure that everyone feels safe in doing so. The responses can be recorded on a whiteboard or flip chart, as appropriate, and you can also highlight any similarities and differences in the responses. The idea is to begin to encourage a deeper level of thinking around the key issues via the process of cooperative idea-sharing.

The key question for this session is: Henry Ford said that the only bad mistake is the one we don't learn from. Do you agree with him?

Case Study & questions for discussion

Vernon is feeling fed up, but also knows that he has learnt a very basic and useful lesson. He has always been good at art and has spent a huge amount of time on this, because he enjoys it so much and gets a real buzz from producing good stuff. The problem is that he didn't spend enough time on doing his maths work as he finds this boring – really boring. Unfortunately, he needs to get maths to go to college to study art, so it was not a good move to get into the habit of spending all day working on his mixed media portfolio and none at all on his maths revision.

When he then failed the maths mock, he felt really bad and his teacher and his mum were really furious with him. His mum said that it's not as if he finds it particularly difficult – he simply just couldn't be bothered to schedule the right amount of study time in. Vernon knew she was right, but didn't want to admit to being in the wrong so sulked for a few days. However, when his best friend told him to stop acting like a failure when he still had another chance to prove himself –

after all, it was only the mock exams – he rethought attitude. He decided he would be better off learning from the mistake rather than ignoring it, so drew up a proper revision timetable for the real exam and kept to the plan.

- What kind of thoughts do you think Vernon is having now that he has 'learnt' from his mistake?

- What pressure may he still be under at the moment?

- How might the prospect of the 'real' exams be affecting him?

- Is he right to make a proper plan? Where is the evidence for this? Who says that this will work for him?

- Do people always find it possible to learn from their mistakes?

- If you were his friend, what advice would you give him now and what support could you offer him?

- How can he keep on track and keep motivated? What would you suggest?

Activities

9.1 Things That Went Wrong – A Self-Reflection

This activity gives the group a technique to productively reflect on a problem. The idea of finding exceptions is particularly powerful and emanates from solution- focused practice.

Ask the group to form pairs and to each identify a problem of thinking or behaviour that they have had. Using Worksheet 9.1, they can work through the two stages of 'Problem Definition' and 'Using Exceptions' in turn.

First one person should explain their problem. Then their partner should ask the questions on the worksheet to elicit the facts around the problem, in order to separate the person from the problem. They should also look for any strengths and resources that may emerge. Ask your partner how they got through the situation or made things better. Then swap over and repeat.

Next, each person should ask their partner the 'Exceptions' questions that relate to the problem they have pinpointed. Then swap over and repeat.

A key objective of this activity is to illustrate to the group why this way of reflecting on a problem is more constructive and positive than simply presenting the problem.

9.2 A Good Failure!

Discuss in the group how getting things wrong and failing are sometimes difficult for young people (and adults) to manage and cope with. Sometimes we forget that failures can be positive. Henry Ford said that the only bad mistake is the one we don't learn from. Ask everyone to identify a personal failure and then consider what they learnt from this. Did it change their behaviour? Did they learn anything from it? Did they identify ways that they might respond more

Session 9 How to See Failure

positively and effectively next time they encountered the same or a similar situation? These are very useful questions to ask and support a solution-focused approach. Finally, each person can use Worksheet 9.2 to write a postcard to a friend and describe this failure and what they learnt from it.

9.3   Developing the 'Bounce-Back' Factor

Discuss with the group how we all need to be able to 'bounce back' after we have experienced a set-back. We need to develop our resilience and ways of coping with the challenges that we face. Ask everyone to reflect upon situations when they have bounced back. What skills and personal qualities have they used to do this? Who are the significant people who have helped them in the process? Now ask the group to consider these questions and to record their thoughts on Worksheet 9.3 to create their own bounce-back list.

9.4   A Solution-Focused Mind

This final activity of the session encourages the group members to engage in a totally solution-focused activity. Using Worksheet 9.4, ask everyone to identify a specific problem that they currently have and to then list all the ways they could solve this problem. Once they have done this, they swap problems with a partner and then list all the ways they could solve their partner's problems.

Feedback & Reflections

Ask the group to reflect upon what they have learnt in the session, posing the following questions:

- ■ What was useful for you in this session?
- ■ What might have made the session more useful for you?
- ■ What have you learnt about yourself in today's session?
- ■ What have you learnt about others?
- ■ How will you use your knowledge and skills to help yourself and others in the future?

The aim is to ensure that the group are able to reflect upon their knowledge and skills and also specifically to identify how and when they might transfer these into new situations in the future.

9.1 Things that Went Wrong - a Self-Reflection

Find a partner to work with. Each of you can identify a problem of thinking or behaving that you have had.

Work through the following two stages in turn.

Problem definition

Invite your partner to tell you about their problem. Try to elicit factual information, for example, who else is present when the problem occurs? Where/when does it happen? Does it happen all the time, or just occasionally? This helps to separate the person from the problem. Look for strengths and resources that may emerge. You might like to ask them how they get through the situation or make things better.

Swap over and repeat.

Using exceptions

Try out some questions with your partner around this problem situation:

- Tell me about the times when it doesn't happen.

- What about the times when it happens less?

- When does it bother you least?

- When have you been able to avoid/resist the urge to ...?

- What was life like before ...?

Swap over and repeat.

Discuss in the whole group why this way of reflecting on a problem is more constructive and positive than simply presenting the problem?

9.2 A Good Failure!

Sometimes we forget that failures can be positive. Henry Ford said that the only bad mistake is the one we don't learn from.

Stop and think! Identify a personal failure and then consider what you learnt from this. Did it change your behaviour? Did you learn anything from it? Did you identify ways that you might respond more positively and effectively next time you encounter the same or a similar situation?

Write to a friend on the postcard and describe this failure and what you learnt from it.

Dear _____

9.3 Developing the 'Bounce-Back' Factor

We all need to be able to 'bounce back' after we have experienced a setback! We need to develop our resilience and ways of coping with the challenges that we face. How have you bounced back? What skills and personal qualities have you used to do this? Who are the significant people who have helped you in the process? Think about these and then record them on the bounce-back list!

My bounce-back list!

9.4 A Solution-Focused Mind

Being Solution-Focused - Focus on Solutions, not Problems!

Think of a problem that you have, and then try and come up with as many ways as possible that you might be able to solve it.

My problem is: _____

_____

Now think of all the ways you could SOLVE this problem.

I could solve this by ...

1 _____

_____

2 _____

_____

3 _____

_____

4 _____

_____

5 _____

_____

6 _____

_____

7 _____

_____

8 _____

_____

9 _____

_____

10 _____

_____

NEXT STEP

Ask someone else how you could solve the problem. Record their ideas on the reverse of the sheet.

Session 10

Test Your Thinking

Introduction & Aims

In this session the focus is primarily on supporting the group to further recognise and understand their ineffective thinking habits and the need to be proactive in learning from them, and on developing our skills and strategies in terms of being able to bounce back. Developing our skills in testing NATs and challenging our thinking by collating the real facts are key essentials in terms of maintaining effective thinking and behaviours, both in the short and longer term. We need to learn how to focus more on the evidence and move away from ineffective thinking that is not truly grounded in reality.

The key aims are as follows:

- For group members to be given the opportunity to further reflect upon why is it important to challenge our negative thoughts and have further opportunities to develop their skills in recognising and challenging ineffective thinking.

- To provide the group members with activities to further develop empathy and their awareness of the similarities and differences in terms of how individuals experience and interpret events.

- To further reflect upon the true and false things that we have all thought about ourselves and to rationally collate and interpret the evidence for and evidence against these thoughts.

- For group members to make use of the Test Your Thinking Grid (Worksheet 10.4), identifying what they would say to their best friend if they had this thought, what their friend would also say to them about this thought and, finally, to assess how much they now believe this thought after having collated more of the evidence. Group members will hopefully be able to begin to make the 'cognitive shift' in terms of recognising the thinking error they have been, or are currently, making.

Warm-up Activity

The warm-up activity is a circle game entitled 'Word Association'. It is designed to get the session going by encouraging everyone to relax and have a bit of fun. Explain that the group members should think freely about other words that come to mind when they think of 'love'. Depending on the group, it may be necessary to set limits on the kind of words that are permissible. After a minute or two, begin the chain. Each person should generate a word that has

Session 10 Test Your Thinking

not been used before until the circle is complete. Several rounds can be played and new chains might include:

- Words that describe how we feel when we love someone/something.
- Words that describe objects, ideas of experiences that we love.
- Songs with the word 'love' in the title.

Icebreaker – A Question to Thought-Storm

The group can be asked to focus upon a key question in order to prompt thinking and awareness around some of the most important issues to be covered in this session. It will be essential to encourage everyone to participate and generate their own responses, but also to ensure that everyone feels safe in doing so. The responses can be recorded on a whiteboard or flip chart, as appropriate, and you can also highlight any similarities and differences in the responses. The idea is to begin to encourage a deeper level of thinking around the key issues via the process of cooperative idea-sharing.

The key question for this session is: Why is it important to challenge our negative thoughts?

Case Study & Questions for Discussion

David has been having a few problems at school just lately. It started with the science teacher who always seemed to be getting at him and trying to put him down in front of the rest of the class. David basically just thought that it was because the teacher wasn't a particularly nice person and seemed to get a kick out of winding him up. He noticed that he did it to other kids in the group as well. However, this last month it seems that the other teachers are also starting to get at him – it's like they are all following the science teacher's lead. In nearly every lesson David seems to have been told off for even the smallest thing, like not having his tie on properly or not looking at the teacher. He's beginning to think that they all hate him and want him out of the school, and part of him is thinking that if they think he is that bad then he might as well just act up to it – at least he'd get a laugh from the others.

- What kind of thoughts do you think David is having?
- What are the main pressures for him at the moment?
- Is he right about his teachers? Do they all hate him?
- What kind of ineffective thinking is he engaging in? Where is the evidence for this?
- Is he right to think that he should start to act up in class? What is the evidence for this?
- How would you find out what the teachers really thought of him and why might this kind of behavioural experiment be a good idea in this situation?
- If you were his friend, what advice would you give him?
- How can he break this cycle of ineffective thinking and behaving, and where can he get the best help?

Activities

10.1 What Would You Feel and Think?

Ask the group to discuss the scenarios on Worksheet 10.1 and to consider how they would feel and think in each of the situations. Divide into small groups and thought-storm ideas together, focusing on the following questions: Do you agree with each other's views? Do we all feel the same or do we respond differently? How would we cope best in each of these somewhat stress-inducing situations?

Bring the whole group together to discuss responses, and emphasise the fact that everyone responds differently to a range of triggers, but that our coping mechanisms can very often be similar and that supporting each other in order to articulate and develop these can be a very helpful strategy.

10.2 True & False Things I Have Thought About Myself

Ask the group to think about some of the things that they have thought about themselves – both in the present and in the past – and to then consider the evidence for and against these thoughts. Using Worksheet 10.2, record these thoughts and the evidence to support them.

What do people notice about the evidence for each thought? The aim of this activity is to reinforce the fact that when we really believe something negative about ourselves, it is often easy to provide a great deal of evidence for the thought. However, when we unpick the evidence for the false things we have thought about ourselves, we can also find a good deal of evidence to support the opposite, more positive, view.

Ultimately, if we believe something is true or false we will have made our minds up over time and gathered the evidence. This is why it is always important to seek out the advice of others and ask if they would agree with our judgements – do they think there is enough evidence to support our views?

10.3 Evidence For & Against

This activity shows the group a very useful strategy for examining the evidence for negative automatic thoughts (NATS) or core beliefs. By using this strategy systematically, they should be able to make a cognitive shift from negative to more positive thinking. In identifying what their friend would say to them if they hear this thought, they are, in essence, writing their own more positive script, and this should be used to replace the existing negative narrative that they have adopted. Worksheet 10.3 provides an example of a NAT and the evidence for and against it. Ask everyone to think of one of their own core beliefs and to follow the same procedure of evidence and questions. The question sequence is as follows:

1   What is the evidence 'for' this thought?

2   What is the evidence 'against' this thought?

3   What would my best friend say if they heard my thought?

4   What would my teacher say if they heard my thought?

5   What would my parent/carer say if they heard my thought?

6   What would I say to my best friend if they had this thought?

7   Am I making any 'thinking' mistakes? (For example: blowing it up, forgetting my strengths or good points, self-blaming or predicting failure, imagining that I know what others are thinking, and so on.)

10.4   Test Your Thinking Grid

This activity both reinforces and builds upon the previous one. Worksheet 10.4 enables group members to identify four key NATs and make use of the 'best friend' strategy to measure the impact of evidence with a trusted person. They can make use of the grid provided, recording their ideas and responses under the different headings.

Feedback & Reflections

Ask the group to reflect upon what they have learnt in the session, posing the following questions:

- What was useful for you in this session?
- What might have made the session more useful for you?
- What have you learnt about yourself in today's session?
- What have you learnt about others?
- How will you use your knowledge and skills to help yourself and others in the future?

The aim is to ensure that the group are able to reflect upon their knowledge and skills and also specifically to identify how and when they might transfer these into new situations in the future.

10.1 What Would You Feel and Think?

Reflection 4 Problem-Solving Situation Cards

How would you feel and think in each of these situations? Work in a small group and thought-storm your ideas. Do you agree with each other's views? Do we all feel the same or do we respond differently?

It is 9.00 pm. You are walking home from your friend's house and someone is following you. How do you feel?	You are the only person in your form that cannot go on the outward bound trip, because your mum can't afford to pay. How do you feel?
Your maths teacher has accused you of cheating in a test and you know that you didn't. How do you feel?	Your best friend has recently put on a lot of weight and is feeling down about herself. She doesn't want to go out or have anything to do with you. How do you feel?
Your older brother has joined a gang and you know that they are all into soft drugs and shoplifting. He says it's none of your business. How do you feel?	Your mum has got a new boyfriend. He continually moans at you for not being tidy around the house and says you're lazy. How do you feel?
Your gran died last week. You were really close to her and used to go shopping with her every Saturday. How do you feel?	You have just found out that your sister has won a million pounds on the lottery. How do you feel?
Your dad has just left home and gone to live with his girlfriend, leaving you and your sister to live with your mum. How do you feel?	The exams start next week and you know that you haven't done enough revision. How do you feel?

- ▨ Discuss in smaller groups and then feedback your ideas to the whole group.
- ▨ How would you cope 'best' in each situation?

10.2 True & False Things I Have Thought about Myself

Think about true and false beliefs that you have held about yourself, both in the past and now. Then think hard about the evidence for and against these thoughts and record this below.

True	False	Evidence for	Evidence against

What do you notice about the evidence for each thought?

10.3 Evidence For & Against

It can be helpful to try and think about our NATs and Core Beliefs from another person's point of view. This can often lead use to a more positive outcome and way of thinking that can replace the original negative thought. Use the questions below to examine one of your NATs or Core Beliefs. First, list the evidence for and against, and then try to answer the questions that follow.

Example:
My NAT or Core Belief: 'They'll laugh at me, and I won't be able to cope.'

Evidence for	Evidence against
People have done it before.	Not everyone is like the bullies at school. They were nice to David. They're all different from each other, and they get on OK. So what if they do? I'll get over it.

- What is the evidence 'for' this thought?

- What is the evidence 'against' this thought?

- What would my best friend say if they heard my thought?

- What would my teacher say if they heard my thought?

- What would my parent/carer say if they heard my thought?

- What would I say to my best friend if they had this thought?

Am I making any 'thinking' mistakes? (For example: blowing it up, forgetting my strengths or good points, self-blaming or predicting failure, imagining that I know what others are thinking, and so on.)

10.4 Test Your Thinking Grid

Using the grid below, examine your four key NATs by considering what your best friend would say to you, and what you would say to your best friend if they had this thought. Now think again about your NAT and rate how strongly you believe it.

THOUGHT	What would my best friend say to me?	What I would say to my best friend if they had this thought?	How much do I believe this thought now, on a scale of 1 to 10? (10 = totally)
(1)			
(2)			
(3)			
(4)			

My Wants & SMART Targets

Introduction & Aims

In this session the focus is primarily on supporting the group to further understand the importance of identifying the 'real' targets that we have in our lives and how to ensure that these can be met in truly practical terms. They are encouraged to see that identifying what we really want for ourselves and others in our lives is an extremely powerful strategy. We also need to be realistic in terms of identifying the small steps that we need to take in order to be able to achieve these goals.

The key aims are as follows:

- To support the group members in understanding how important it is for us to have a vision for our lives and to make goals that we can work towards that are realistic and time-bound.

- To introduce the group members to the concept of ambivalence and the fact that this state can actually prevent us from moving forwards, so that we may become stuck in our behaviours or negative patterns of thinking.

- For group members to be able to identify and articulate what their ideal world might look like and how they would behave, feel and think in such a world. How would those around them also behave, feel and think? The aim is to highlight and articulate what would be different, positive and wonderful about this world.

- To ensure that group members can identify their key 'wants' for their lives – thinking about things that they would like to change or might like to do differently, things that they would want less of, or more of, in their lives.

- To understand that being able to prioritise these 'wants' is also an essential skill when building a healthy future that promotes and ensures well-being.

- To ensure that the group members understand what a 'SMART' target looks like, and to engage them in the process of formulating these.

Warm-up Activity

This warm-up is called the 'Post-It Note Guessing Game'. Pick one name for each person playing. Do not let any of the players see the names until the game starts.

- ■ The names should represent real people group members are likely to know (celebrities, animated characters, storybook characters, and so on). Some examples could be: Cheryl Cole, Harry Styles, Rihanna, Kate Middleton, Harry Potter, Maggie Simpson and Zac Efron.

- ■ Stick one post-it note on each player's forehead. Do not allow them to see the name before you put it there.

- ■ Each person gets 20 'yes' or 'no' questions to find out who they are. For example, the initial question is often, 'Am I female?', or 'Am I male?'

- ■ The players have to roam around the room to ask other players the questions. They cannot ask only one player all the questions; the point is to mingle. Whoever guesses their name first, using 20 or fewer questions, wins the game.

Icebreaker - A Question to Thought-Storm

The group can be asked to focus upon a key question in order to prompt thinking and awareness around some of the most important issues to be covered in this session. It will be essential to encourage everyone to participate and generate their own responses, but also to ensure that everyone feels safe in doing so. The responses can be recorded on a whiteboard or flip chart, as appropriate, and you can also highlight any similarities and differences in the responses. The idea is to begin to encourage a deeper level of thinking around the key issues via the process of cooperative idea-sharing.

The key question for this session is: Is it important for us to have a vision for our lives and to make goals that we can work towards?

Case Study & Questions for Discussion

Cathy wants to be a super model like Kate Moss and Naomi Campbell. She spends as much time as possible looking at magazines and reading about them, as well as comparing herself and her looks with them, which is starting to be a bit of a problem. She is beginning to feel down about her own chances of achieving this goal. She knows that they have more money and access to plastic surgery – and the best people to help them to look good, such as make-up artists and hairdressers. Her mum keeps telling her to get a grip and that, although she's nice looking, this is actually an unrealistic goal, because she is short and doesn't have the kind of body that the agencies seem to want. She says that what Cathy needs to do is just to be happy with what she's got and go to college to do a beauty course, since at least that would give her a good job in the future. Cathy won't believe her mum and thinks that she's just being unkind.

- ■ What kind of thoughts do you think Cathy is having?

- ■ What are the main pressures for her at the moment and where do these pressures come from?

- How might the prospect of not being able to achieve this goal be affecting her?

- Is she right to chase her dream? Where is the evidence for this?

- Is she right to think that she has the qualities needed to be a super model? What is the evidence for this? How could she find out, apart from taking feedback from her mum?

- Do people always have realistic goals?

- If you were her friend, what advice would you give her?

- How can she sort this out and where can she get the best help?

Activities

11.1   Exploring Ambivalence – The Pros & Cons of Making That Change!

Discuss with the group members the concept of ambivalence and the part that this plays in motivating us to change. When we want to change something it is not always easy to do so; sometimes this will be because we 'sort of' want to change – but 'sort of' do not want to change at the same time! It can be difficult, as this state of ambivalence can actually prevent us from moving forwards and we can become stuck in our behaviours or negative patterns of thinking.

Ask everyone to 'Stop, Think and Reflect!', and identify one behaviour that they think they may want to change, but which they are not entirely convinced that they need to alter. Then, using Worksheet 11.1 and the rating scale of 1 to 10 (where 1 is very little, and 10 is totally), ask them to think about how much they want to change and to identify where they are on the scale.

Next, everyone should record the pros and cons of making this change. What will be better or worse for them and other people if they make the change? Finally, ask the group to reflect on the two lists and again consider and rate how much they now want to make this change.

There should be a difference in ratings, as the process of identifying the positives that could result from change should reinforce the need for change – even if the shift is a small one.

11.2   An Ideal World?

Using Worksheet 11.2, ask the group to reflect on the notion of an ideal world or future for themselves and to focus on the following questions:

- What would your ideal world look like?

- How would you behave, feel and think, and how would others behave, feel and think? What would be different, positive and wonderful about it?

They are asked to record their ideas in the picture frame using cartoons or a 'mind map', and then to consider what the obstacles really are to the creation of this perfect world. Are they all impossible to overcome, or can they all be overcome?

11.3   My Five 'Wants'

Give the group members Worksheet 11.3 and explain that in this activity they will identify key goals or 'wants' for themselves by undertaking the staged or stepped approach as follows:

Step 1 Identifying 'wants'

Take a few minutes to think about things that you would like to change in your life. Think about things you might like to do differently, things that you would want less of or more of in your life. Thought-storm these ideas and record your list on a piece of paper.

Step 2 Select your five main 'wants'

Next select the five things you want most and write each of these on a post-it note. Next to each of these 'wants', write down a behaviour that you will have to change or something that you will have to do differently in order to get closer to achieving this want.

Step 3 Prioritise your 'wants'

Decide which of your 'wants' you want to achieve first (your 'top want'), second, third, and so on. Put your post-it 'wants' in the correct order.

Step 4 Discuss with a partner

Questions you can then discuss with a partner:

- How did you decide on your 'top want'?
- What does your partner think about your decision?

11.4   SMART Targets

In this final activity explain to the group that they are going to use Worksheet 11.4 to set themselves SMART targets using the following process:

1 **Small** – a 'small' step, a little hill not a mountain

2 **Measurable** – something for which you can measure success

3 **Attainable** – you can get there and do it

4 **Relevant** – something that really means something to you and is relevant to you

5 **Time-bound** – you have set a review date and know when you will measure your success

When developing their goals the group also need to be able to answer the following six questions:

1 Who will do this/help me?

2 What will be achieved?

3 Where will I do this/get help/do my best?

4 Why am I doing this/making this change?

5 How will I know I am really successful, or if I need to evaluate and try again?

This is a useful and constructive process, which will be transferrable to a range of contexts and problems.

Feedback & Reflections

Ask the group to reflect upon what they have learnt in the session, posing the following questions:

- What was useful for you in this session?

- What might have made the session more useful for you?

- What have you learnt about yourself in today's session?

- What have you learnt about others?

- How will you use your knowledge and skills to help yourself and others in the future?

The aim is to ensure that the group are able to reflect upon their knowledge and skills and also specifically to identify how and when they might transfer these into new situations in the future.

11.1 Exploring Ambivalence: The Pros & Cons of Making that Change!

When we want to change something it is not always easy to do so. Sometimes this will be because we 'sort of' want to change – but 'sort of' don't want to change at the same time! It can be difficult, as this state of ambivalence may actually prevent us from moving forwards and we can become stuck in our behaviours or negative patterns of thinking.

Stop, Think and Reflect!

Identify one behaviour that you think you may want to change, but that you are not entirely convinced that you need to.

On a scale of 1 to 10 (where 1 is very little and 10 is totally), how much do you want to change? Where are you on the scale?

1   2   3   4   5   6   7   8   9   10

NEXT

Record the pros and cons of making this change. What will be better or worse for you and other people if you do this? List your thoughts below.

PROS	CONS
_____	_____
_____	_____
_____	_____
_____	_____
_____	_____
_____	_____
_____	_____
_____	_____
_____	_____

Now rate yourself again for how strongly you want to make this change. Is there a difference and, if so, why do you think this might be?

1   2   3   4   5   6   7   8   9   10

11.2 An Ideal World?

What would your ideal world look like?

How would you behave, feel and think, and how would others behave, feel and think?

What would be different, positive and wonderful about it?

Record your ideas in the picture frame using cartoons or a 'mind map', and then consider what the obstacles really are to the creation of this perfect world. Discuss these with a partner.

Are any of the obstacles impossible to overcome, or can they all be overcome?

11.3 My Five Wants

Use the stepped process below to identify the top five things you would like to change in your life.

Step 1   Identifying 'Wants'

Take a few minutes to think about things that you would like to change in your life. Think about things you might like to do differently, things that you would want less of, or more of, in your life. Thought-storm these ideas and record your list on a piece of paper.

Step 2   Select Your Five Main 'Wants'

Next select the five things you want most and write each of these on a post-it note. Next to each of these, then write down a behaviour that you will have to change or something that you will have to do differently in order to get closer to achieving this want.

Step 3   Prioritise Your 'Wants'

Decide which of your 'wants' you want to achieve first (your 'top want'), second, third, and so on. Put your post-it 'wants' in the correct order.

Step 4   Discuss With a Partner

Questions you can then discuss with a partner:

- How did you decide on your 'top want'?

- What does your partner think about your decision?

11.4 SMART Targets

Setting SMART targets is a useful way of thinking about your targets and goals.

Is each of your targets or goals for the future ...

Small – a 'small' step, a little hill, not a mountain?

Measurable – something for which you can measure your success?

Attainable – something that you know you can actually do?

Relevant – something that really means something to you and is relevant to you?

Time bound – something for which you can set a review date, when you measure your success?

When developing your goal you need to be able to answer the following questions:

1   Who will do this/help me?

_____

_____

2   What will be achieved?

_____

_____

3   Where will I do this/get help/do my best?

_____

_____

4   Why am I doing this/making this change?

_____

_____

5   How will I know I am really successful or if I need to re-evaluate and try again?

_____

_____

Building Positive Thinking Habits

Introduction & Aims

In this session the focus is primarily on supporting the group to further build upon their skills of positive thinking and to be able to move farther away from ineffective and negative patterns of thinking, feeling and behaving. They are encouraged to see how identifying the skills and strategies of a positive thinker is extremely powerful. We also need to be able to make use of a range of methods to ensure that we maintain a positive and solution-focused outlook on life and prevent our 'bad moods' from taking over and impacting negatively on our state of mind.

The key aims are as follows:

- For group members to be able to identify the qualities, skills and attributes of a positive thinker and to further reflect upon their own skills at this present moment in time.

- To ensure that group members are able to identify what they value and appreciate about those who are significant to them and to understand the importance of being able to articulate this.

- To support group members in being able to identify the positive to negative ratio of their thought processes on a daily basis, and to understand the need to ensure a healthy balance between both. For group members to also practise how to calculate the 'happiness ratio' for each day and to consider what this suggests about them and the way they live and experience their lives.

- To be able to recognise when they feel a bad mood starting and that there are six things they can do to stop it taking over.

- To recognise the need to always acknowledge the positives in their lives and to understand the impact that such a 'happy habit' has on their well-being and mental health.

Session 12   Building Positive Thinking Habits

warm-up Activity

The warm-up activity is for group members to swap seats with each other by making simple decisions. For example, 'Swap seats if you like/don't like ...'

- chocolate
- broccoli
- pop music
- classical music
- PE
- science
- geography

Icebreaker - A Question to Thought-Storm

The group can be asked to focus upon a key question in order to prompt thinking and awareness around some of the most important issues to be covered in this session. It will be essential to encourage everyone to participate and generate their own responses, but also to ensure that everyone feels safe in doing so. The responses can be recorded on a whiteboard or flip chart, as appropriate, and you can also highlight any similarities and differences in the responses. The idea is to begin to encourage a deeper level of thinking around the key issues via the process of cooperative idea-sharing.

The key question for this session is: What are the qualities, skills and attributes of a positive thinker?

Case Study 4 Questions for Discussion

Hamid has a problem with getting himself out of a bad mood. It seems that when he begins to feel down, it's like there's nothing that he can do about this. He just goes up to his room and stares out of the window. Then he goes online and looks at what everyone else is doing and saying on Facebook. They always seem to be doing really interesting stuff and their lives seem so much better and more exciting than his. They have a laugh all the time, while he is just left on his own feeling down. He knows that he should probably try to do something else in order to be able to shake himself out of it, but is beginning to think that this will never be possible as everyone else knows what a bore he is and that his life is just such a boring one compared to theirs. No one will want to know him or have anything to do with him. So, he keeps to the same routine and goes to his room, getting more and more down and feeling more and more isolated.

- What kind of thoughts do you think Hamid is having?
- What are the main pressures he seems to be experiencing at the moment and where do these come from?
- How might his routine for coping with bad moods be affecting him? Why is this counterproductive?

- Is he right about thinking everyone else has a brilliant and interesting life? Where is the evidence for this?

- Is he right to compare himself to others?

- Do people have to learn how to cope with a mood and recognise when it is rational or not? What might be the benefits of being able to do this?

- If you were his friend, what advice would you give him?

- How can he break this cycle and where can he get the best help?

Activities

12.1   Beyond Appearance

Explain to the group that you want them to think beyond a person's outward appearance and to identify the specific qualities that they have which make them special and unique. Ask them to write the name of somebody they love on the name-plate of the trophy on Worksheet 12.1. They need to try to focus on what impresses them about this person. What are their talents? What are their achievements? What do they value about them? They can write any ideas in the area surrounding the trophy.

12.2   Daily Diary

This diary activity is intended to help people to reflect upon how positive they are about themselves and their world, and to think more about the need to increase the ratio of positive to negative experiences in their lives.

Using Worksheet 12.2, they can keep a daily diary for one week and then record and count the positive and negative words or phrases they have used for each day's events. Then they should calculate their 'happiness ratio' for each day, using the ratio symbol. For instance, 4 positive thoughts to 2 negative thoughts is a ratio of 4 to 2 (4:2). Finally, ask the group to consider what this suggests about them and the way they live and experience their lives.

12.3   Bust a Mood!

Worksheet 12.3 provides a series of strategies that are intended to support the maintenance of positive thinking. It is important that people try to prevent negative thoughts from taking over and increasing a potential bad mood. The worksheet lists six things they can do to stop it taking over, as follows:

1   Catch the thought …
What can you say to yourself to stop that bad mood from getting worse?

2   Act fast …
What one thing can you do now to begin to sort out the situation so that it doesn't get worse?

Session 12   Building Positive Thinking Habits

3   Distract yourself …
Take your mind off it. Talk about something else with a friend. How can you make that happen? What can you discuss that will help change your mood?

4   Do something different …
Change your activity. What can you do now to get your mind off the situation that has prompted your bad mood?

5   Complete an act of kindness.
Do something for someone else. When people do things for other people they have more meaning in their lives and feel better than when they do things for themselves. What could you do?

6   Exercise
Get moving. Take some exercise so that you can't think about that bad mood. What will you do?

Working in pairs, try to identify four further strategies that people can use. In the whole group people can share their ideas and what works for them.

12.4   Positive Post-Its!

This activity is designed to reinforce positive thinking and the importance of 'catching' our positive thoughts. It is another useful strategy, which can be used time and time again.

Explain to the group that, for one week, every time they have a positive thought about themselves or someone else, they should record it on a post-it note and then stick these onto Worksheet 12.4. Then, at the end of the week, they can read through all of the notes and reflect upon how this makes them feel.

Feedback & Reflections

Ask the group to reflect upon what they have learnt in the session, posing the following questions:

- What was useful for you in this session?
- What might have made the session more useful for you?
- What have you learnt about yourself in today's session?
- What have you learnt about others?
- How will you use your knowledge and skills to help yourself and others in the future?

The aim is to ensure that the group are able to reflect upon their knowledge and skills and also specifically to identify how and when they might transfer these into new situations in the future.

12.1 Beyond Appearance

It is important to think beyond the outward appearance of a person and to identify the specific qualities that make them special and unique.

Write the name of somebody you love on the name-plate of the trophy.

Try to focus on what impresses you about this person.

What are their talents? What are their achievements? What do you value about them?

Write any ideas in the area surrounding the trophy.

12.2 Daily Diary

Keep a daily diary for one week and then record and count the positive and negative words and phrases you have used for each day's events.

Calculate your 'happiness ratio' for each day by writing the positive against the negative using the ratio symbol. For instance, 4 positive thoughts to 2 negative thoughts is a ratio of 4 to 2 (4:2). Think about what this suggests about you and the way you live and experience your life.

Day	Positive words/ phrases	Negative words/phrases	Happiness ratio	What does this say about me?
Sunday				
Monday				
Tuesday				
Wednesday				
Thursday				
Friday				
Saturday				

12.3 Bust a Mood!

When you feel a bad mood starting, here are six things you can do to stop it taking over:

1 Catch the thought ...
What can you say to yourself to stop that bad mood from getting worse?

2 Act fast ...
What one thing can you do now to begin to sort out the situation so that it doesn't get worse?

3 Distract yourself ...
Take your mind off it. Talk about something else with a friend. How can you make that happen? What can you discuss that will help change your mood?

4 Do something different ...
Change your activity. What can you do now to get your mind off the situation that has prompted your bad mood?

5 Complete an act of kindness.
Do something for someone else. When people do things for other people they have more meaning in their lives and feel better than when they do things for themselves. What could you do?

6 Exercise
Get moving. Take some exercise so that you can't think about that bad mood. What will you do?

Work with a partner to identify four more strategies you can use.

1 _____

_____

2 _____

_____

3 _____

_____

4 _____

_____

12.4 Positive Post-Its!

For one week, every time you have a positive thought about yourself or someone else, record it on a post-it note!

Stick them onto this sheet and then, at the end of the week, read them all through and reflect upon how this makes you feel!

Session 13
Chillax!

Introduction & Aims

In this session the focus is primarily on supporting the group to further build upon their skills in terms of managing stress and anxiety by using specific tools of relaxation. They are encouraged to identify the strategies that work for them and to also make use of these on a regular basis in order to develop a habit of healthy relaxation.

The key aims are as follows:

- For group members to be able to identify how they relax and why is it important to be able to maintain a balance between relaxation and work.

- To be able to make use of visualisation techniques in order to feel safe and calm and to foster positive thinking.

- For group members to consider how being able to meditate can support well-being and to develop their ability to meditate, freeing themselves from negative or over-busy thinking.

- For group members to be able to make use of a relaxation script in order to reduce stress and anxiety and to judge if this is an effective tool for them in order to promote a sense of peace and well-being.

- To encourage group members to devise and make use of a relaxation plan and to try to stick to this, in order to ensure a balance between rest, work and play.

Warm-up Activity

The ground rules are reinforced at the beginning of the session to help the group feel safer and to ensure that everyone shares their thoughts and feelings at their own comfort level. The activity is introduced using the circle-time tool, 'Silent Statements', which allows people to share information without the pressure of having to speak. You may wish to prepare an opening statement as follows:

Today we will be communicating and sharing without talking. I will say something ... for example, 'I like football'. If it is true for you, then raise your hand. Nobody should speak, but I would like you to look around the group and notice who has raised their hand. If you are the only person who has raised their hand, that's fine. We're here to help each other

... remember that we said we would ... [quote ground rule]. If it is true for you, but you do not want to join in, then don't raise your hand – but try and participate, even if it is in your own head. Please remember that we speak only for ourselves. If someone passes, it is not your business to tell the group something they have not chosen to tell us.

Begin this activity with 'low risk' statements, such as 'I have a pet,' or 'I like chocolate,' to encourage people to feel comfortable about sharing. It is important that this activity is done in silence.

Choose a selection from the following statements. They are written from low risk to high risk and back to low risk:

- I don't like coming to school.
- Sometimes I feel stressed.
- I have lain awake at night worrying about things.
- I have seen a website about anorexia.
- I have a friend who self-harms.
- Someone close to me has died.
- Someone close to me has suffered from depression.
- My parents sometimes argue.
- I like myself.
- I often have arguments with my friends.
- I have a good friend I can talk to.
- I feel happy at home.

Thank everyone for taking part in this activity and summarise some facts and figures about the group. (A helper may take notes during the activity.) For example: five people don't like coming to school; two people have seen a website about anorexia

Icebreaker – A Question to Thought-Storm

The group can be asked to focus upon a key question in order to prompt thinking and awareness around some of the most important issues to be covered in this session. It will be essential to encourage everyone to participate and generate their own responses, but also to ensure that everyone feels safe in doing so. The responses can be recorded on a whiteboard or flip chart, as appropriate, and you can also highlight any similarities and differences in the responses. The idea is to begin to encourage a deeper level of thinking around the key issues via the process of cooperative idea-sharing.

The key question for this session is: How do we relax and why is it important to be able to maintain a balance between relaxation and work?

Session 13   Chillax!

Case Study 4 Questions for Discussion

Cheryl just can't seem to relax. She is always worrying about things and thinks that if she doesn't work hard all the time or do something worthwhile, then she's just simply not good enough and not really being a good person. It is worst when she goes to bed at night and tries to sleep. She just can't seem to switch her thoughts off at all. She's told her mum, who just laughed and said she was like that until she left school and got a job and was having to work so hard that she just fell asleep without thinking. She told Cheryl that she will grow out of it, but Cheryl doesn't really believe her and feels tired all the time. She has tried to listen to music last thing, but it doesn't make her sleepy – it just seems to turn the volume up in her head.

- What kind of thoughts do you think Cheryl is having?

- What are the main pressures she seems to be experiencing at the moment and where do these come from?

- How might her core beliefs be affecting her? Why is this counterproductive?

- Is she right in thinking that working hard all the time makes you a good person or shows that you are one? Where is the evidence for this?

- Is her mum's advice useful or not?

- Do people have to learn how to switch off and relax? What might be the benefits of being able to do this?

- If you were her friend, what advice would you give her?

- How can she break this cycle and where can she get the best help?

Activities

13.1   A Place of Peace

This is a visualisation exercise and can be very useful as an aid to the relaxation process. Ask the group to visualise a place of peace in which they can truly relax and not have to manage the intrusion of negative thoughts. While doing so, ask them to consider the following questions: what does your place look, feel, smell and sound like? Everyone should try to conjure up this image in their mind and then record it in the form of a 'mind map' on Worksheet 13.1.

Finally, ask everyone to consider the following questions:

- When could you use this image to reduce stress and anxiety levels?

- When would it work best?

To end, form pairs and discuss ideas with partners and then feedback to the group as a whole if time permits.

13.2   Meditate

Give the group the meditation exercise on Worksheet 13.2 and ask them to try this out for themselves. It is important to emphasise the need to undertake this exercise in a quiet and relaxing atmosphere and also to highlight the fact that, as with any such skill, the more we practise it, the more skilled and competent we become. Encourage everyone to use the script to support them in developing their ability to meditate and free themselves from negative or over-busy thinking.

13.3 Chillax!

Give the group the relaxation exercise on Worksheet 13.3 and ask them to try it out for themselves. It is important to emphasise the need to undertake this exercise in a quiet and relaxing atmosphere and also to highlight the fact that, as with any such skill, the more we are proactive and use it, the more skilled and competent we become. Encourage everyone to use the script to support them to develop their ability to meditate and free themselves from negative or over-busy thinking. Explain that in this activity they need to think about tensing each of the major muscle groups in their bodies for about 5 to 10 seconds and then relaxing them.

13.4 My Relaxation Plan

Ask the group to devise a personal relaxation plan and, in particular, to attempt to use some of the key skills and relaxation strategies they have learned so far. There are two steps to this task.

Step 1 Ask everyone to start by thought-storming what makes them relax and feel calm. They can draw this as a 'mind map' on Worksheet 13.4.

Step 2 Next, everyone should try to make a relaxation plan. They should identify their three most stressful situations, and think about the strategies they would use to try and keep more calm and relaxed in each of the situations. Now they can try these out when they next encounter one of the situations.

It may be helpful to allocate some time at the start of the next session to review these plans and discuss how well people's chosen strategies have worked or otherwise.

Feedback & Reflections

Ask the group to reflect upon what they have learnt in the session, posing the following questions:

- What was useful for you in this session?
- What might have made the session more useful for you?
- What have you learnt about yourself in today's session?
- What have you learnt about others?
- How will you use your knowledge and skills to help yourself and others in the future?

The aim is to ensure that the group are able to reflect upon their knowledge and skills and also specifically to identify how and when they might transfer these into new situations in the future.

13.1 A Place of Peace

Being able to visualise a place of peace can help you to relax and reduce stress.

Think about your own peaceful place where you feel safe and calm, and where you do not have to deal with intrusive thoughts.

What does your place look, feel, smell and sound like? Try and create a clear image in your head, and then record it as a 'mind map' below.

Now consider the following questions:

- When could you use this image to reduce stress and anxiety levels?
- When would it work best?

Discuss your ideas with a partner.

13.2 Meditate

You can use this meditation script to help develop your ability to meditate and free yourself from negative or over-busy thinking. It is important to carry out this exercise in a quiet and relaxing atmosphere – and remember, the more you practise and use this technique, the more skilled and competent you will become.

Feel all of your attention gently falling from the top of your head down to your neck, lightly falling like a snowflake or a leaf falling from a tree. Feel your attention move down through your shoulders ... your arms ... your hands ... your chest and stomach ... your hips and thighs ... your knees and ankles ... into your feet and all the way down to your toes. Let your mind rest in your body, noticing all the feelings inside – tingling, shivers, warmth, coolness, relaxation, tightness – or nothing at all. Notice how the sensations and feelings change when you bring attention to them. See if you can feel the stillness in your body as you sit, not moving, and noticing changing sensations throughout your body.

Adapted from Goodman (2005, p. 217)

13.3 Chillax!

You can use this relaxation script to help develop your ability to meditate and free yourself from negative or over-busy thinking. It is important to carry out this exercise in a quiet and relaxing atmosphere – and remember, the more you practise this technique, the more skilled and competent you will become.

Tense each of the major muscle groups in your body for about 5 to 10 seconds and then RELAX. Some parts of your body may be more tense than others. Try to find these and pay more attention to them.

PRACTISE! PRACTISE! PRACTISE!

▓ Choose a quiet, warm and comfortable place.

▓ Sit in a comfy chair or lie on your bed.

▓ Make sure you won't be disturbed.

▓ Tense the muscles in ...

(a) your arms   (e) your shoulders

(b) your hands   (f) your neck

(c) your legs and feet   (g) your face

(d) your stomach

▓ Tense each group of muscles for 5 to 10 seconds and then relax.

▓ Repeat for another group of muscles.

▓ Close your eyes and count slowly to 100.

13.4 My Relaxation Plan

My personal relaxation strategies

Step 1

Thought-storm! What makes me relax and feel calm?

Draw this as a 'mind map'.

```



```

Step 2

Now, try to make a relaxation plan. Identify your three most stressful situations:

1 _____

2 _____

3 _____

Think about the strategies you would use to try and keep more calm and relaxed in each of the situations. Think about the strategies and techniques you have learned so far.

_____

_____

Try these out when you next encounter one of these stressful situations.

Session 14
Positive Selfie

Introduction & Aims

In this session the focus is primarily on supporting the group to further build upon their skill in managing negative feelings and thoughts by homing in specifically on the positives – including their own strengths, skills and positive attributes. They are encouraged to identify the strategies that work for them and to also make use of these on a regular basis in order to develop the habit of positive thinking.

The key aims are as follows:

- For group members to consider how we can keep a positive attitude and remain motivated even when things go wrong in our lives.

- To practise using peer support to identify and build on strengths and to understand what a useful and helpful process this is.

- For group members to have the opportunity to make up their own self-awareness profile by listing their ideas under each of the 'seven selves' headings. They can also then reflect on the accuracy of their judgements – identifying if they see themselves as others see them and the accuracy of their self-awareness and thinking.

- To make use of a problem-solving framework in seven steps in order to focus further on solutions and see how it is easier to remain motivated and positive if we identify the smaller steps towards the end result.

- For group members to engage in the 'I'm a winner' and the positive selfie activities in order to further reinforce their positive attributes and to understand that they can use such strategies and tools to boost their positive feelings when they do feel down or demotivated.

Warm-Up Activity

The warm-up for this session is called 'Sparkling Moments'. Divide the group into pairs. Each person should describe to their partner a 'sparkling moment' they have had. This is a moment when something has gone really well for them. This may be at school or home whilst spending time with friends. They should spend no more than three minutes describing their sparkling moment and should focus on:

Session 14   Positive Selfie

- What made it a sparkling moment for them?
- How did they feel when they had their sparkling moment?
- Who else might have noticed?

Icebreaker - A Question to Thought-Storm

The group can be asked to focus upon a key question in order to prompt thinking and awareness around some of the most important issues to be covered in this session. It will be essential to encourage everyone to participate and generate their own responses, but also to ensure that everyone feels safe in doing so. The responses can be recorded on a whiteboard or flip chart, as appropriate, and you can also highlight any similarities and differences in the responses. The idea is to begin to encourage a deeper level of thinking around the key issues via the process of cooperative idea-sharing.

The key question for this session is: How do we keep a positive attitude and remain motivated even when things go wrong?

Case Study & Questions for Discussion

Kelly does not feel that she has any real strengths. She continually compares herself to her friends and classmates and thinks that they are all more talented, better looking and happier than she is. She has never won a competition, come first in a test, or got the highest marks in an end of year exam. She did get a special mention in an assembly for being kind to a new student who was lonely and feeling left out, and also for being helpful in the dining hall and looking after the younger students when they entered year 7 and didn't know the routines and systems. However, she does not think that these are strengths and just wants to be the 'best' at something. She thinks that she can never really be truly happy unless she is first or the best and does not think that either thing will ever happen to her.

- What kind of thoughts do you think Kelly is having?
- What is the kind of ineffective thinking she is engaging in?
- What are the main pressures she seems to be experiencing at the moment, and where do these come from?
- How might her core beliefs be affecting her? Why is this counterproductive?
- Is she right in thinking that she has no real strengths? Where is the evidence for this? Where is the evidence against this?
- Do people have to be the 'best' to be truly happy in this life?
- Does trying to be the best that we can be help us to be more successful and happy?
- If you were her friend, what advice would you give her at this point in time?
- How can she break this cycle and where can she get the best help?

Activities

14.1   Identifying Strengths – A Job for Two!

Ask the group to form pairs and then to decide who is going to speak and who will listen.

The speaker should begin by briefly describing a recent piece of schoolwork that has gone well.

The listener should now question the speaker to help them identify the skills, talents or special qualities they used to help them in this achievement. They should try to be a tough interviewer to make the speaker name as many of their positive qualities as possible. The listener should list the qualities in the box on Worksheet 14.1.

The listener should next ask the speaker to think about other times in their lives when these skills may be useful.

The listener should now tell the speaker the skills, talents and special qualities they have listed for them and give them the written list on the worksheet.

Swap roles and repeat the activity.

14.2   The Seven Selves of Self-Awareness

Give each person a copy of Worksheet 14.2, which describes the 'Seven Selves of Self-Awareness'. Read through the descriptions and discuss these in the group.

REAL SELF This is us as we see ourselves now! This is about our behaviour, thoughts and feelings as they are in this moment. This self is how we see ourselves at the moment in our social and learning contexts.

IDEAL SELF This is who and what we would like to be. This would be the best version of ourselves!

FANTASY SELF This is how we would like to be if reality did not figure or matter and we were not constrained by it – imagine winning the lottery, for example, so that money is not an object.

OPEN SELF This is the self that other people out there notice. For example, what would your friends say about you and how you behave, think and feel?

HIDDEN SELF This is the self that only you know about and others do not. For example, you may be a great dancer, but you are too inhibited or shy to dance in front of others so they will not know this about you.

PRESENT SELF This is you now and how you perceive your strengths and skills. For example, you may say that you are a good listener, or a hard worker or generous.

SELF IN PROGRESS This is the self as it is currently developing – like a work in progress. This may involve identifying something that you would like to be good at, but may find quite hard at the moment. For example, you may wish to feel more confident at speaking out in class, or when meeting new people or when performing in a show.

The next part of the activity requires the group to make up their own self-awareness profiles by listing their ideas under each of the seven headings. Then ask the group to form pairs and discuss ideas with a partner, reflecting in particular on the accuracy of their judgements. Do people see themselves as others see them? They can reflect further on the accuracy of their self-awareness and thinking around this topic.

14.3   Problem-Solve

Explain to the group that they can use the structured format on Worksheet 14.3 to begin to solve their problems. This is a solution-focused approach in which the group are encouraged to visualise life without the problem.

14.4   I'm a Winner!

Give everyone a copy of Worksheet 14.4 to guide them through this activity, which is designed to reinforce positive thinking and to make use of peer support in the process. Ask everyone to work in pairs and decide who is going to talk first and who is going to listen. Explain that the aim is to make use of a structured script as follows:

Speaker: Think back to a time when you have felt positive or proud of yourself. Describe what happened to your partner.

Listener: Listen carefully to your partner. Encourage them by asking questions when appropriate, for example: 'Which qualities or talents helped you to achieve your special moment?'

Now swap roles and repeat the activity!

14.5   A Positive Selfie!

For this activity, ask all of the group members to take selfies and to stick these onto Worksheet 14.5 when they have been printed. It might be useful to ask the group to take these before the session and bring the printouts with them. Next, ask them to write around the edge of the picture, recording all the positives they can think of about themselves and including positive comments from friends and family too. This will help to highlight all of their thinking, feeling and doing habits that are positive and healthy.

Feedback 4 Reflections

Ask the group to reflect upon what they have learnt in the session, posing the following questions:

- What was useful for you in this session?

- What might have made the session more useful for you?

- What have you learnt about yourself in today's session?

- What have you learnt about others?

- How will you use your knowledge and skills to help yourself and others in the future?

The aim is to ensure that the group are able to reflect upon their knowledge and skills and also specifically to identify how and when they might transfer these into new situations in the future.

14.1 Identifying Strengths - A Job for Two!

1 In your pair decide who is going to speak and who will listen.

2 The speaker should start by briefly describing a recent piece of schoolwork that has gone well.

3 The listener can then question the speaker to help them identify the skills, talents or special qualities they have used to help them in this achievement. They should try to be a tough interviewer to make the speaker name as many positive qualities about themselves as possible. List the qualities for the speaker in the box below.

4 The listener can then ask the speaker to think about other times in their lives when these skills might be useful.

5 The listener should now read to the speaker the skills, talents and special qualities they have listed for them and give them the written list.

6 Swap roles and repeat the activity.

Strengths, Skills, Qualities

14.2 The Seven Selves of Self-Awareness

1 Real Self

This is us as we see ourselves now! This is about our behaviour, thoughts and feelings as they are in this moment. This self is how we see ourselves at the moment in our social and learning contexts.

_____

_____

_____

_____

2 Ideal Self

This is who and what we would like to be. This would be the best version of ourselves!

_____

_____

_____

_____

3 Fantasy Self

This is how we would like to be if reality didn't figure or matter and we were not constrained by it – imagine winning the lottery, for example, so that money is not an object.

_____

_____

_____

_____

4 Open Self

This is the self that other people out there notice. For example, what would your friends say about you and how you behave, think and feel?

_____

_____

_____

_____

Page 1 of 2

5 Hidden Self

This is the self that only you know about and others don't. For example, you may be a great dancer, but you are too inhibited or shy to dance in front of others so they won't know this about you.

_____

_____

_____

_____

6 Present Self

This is you now and how you perceive your strengths and skills. For example, you may say that you are a good listener or a hard worker or generous.

_____

_____

_____

_____

7 Self in Progress

This is the self as it is currently developing – like a work in progress. This may involve identifying something that you would like to be good at, but may find quite hard at the moment. For example, you may wish to feel more confident at speaking out in class, or when meeting new people or when performing in a show.

_____

_____

_____

_____

Stop, think and reflect! Create your own self-awareness profile by listing your ideas under each of the seven headings above. Then discuss these with a partner and examine the accuracy of your judgements.

- ■ Do you see yourself as others see you?
- ■ How accurate is your self-awareness and thinking?

Page 2 of 2

14.3 Problem-Solve

Think of a problem that you would like to solve, and work through the steps below to begin find a solution to your problem.

Step 1 Describe the Problem

Step 2 Visualise Life Without the Problem

What would it look like? How would you think, feel and act and how would others respond?

Step 3 TAKE ACTION!

Identify 3 key things you can do in order to reach the state of life without the problem.

1 _____

2 _____

3 _____

Page 1 of 2

Step 4 Identify Resources

Who else could help you? How?

_____

_____

_____

_____

Step 5 Identify Potential Problems and Plan

What would happen if ...?

_____

_____

_____

_____

_____

Step 6 Visualise Success

How will you know when your problem is solved?

_____

_____

_____

_____

_____

Step 7 BE CONFIDENT!

How confident are you now that this problem can be solved if you take action?

_____

_____

_____

_____

GO FOR IT!

14.4 I'm a Winner!

In your pairs decide who is going to talk first and who is going to listen.

Now use the script below to discover more about your skills, talents and qualities.

Speaker: Think back to a time when you have felt positive or proud of yourself. Describe what happened to your partner.

Listener: Listen carefully to your partner. Encourage them by asking questions when appropriate, for example: 'Which qualities or talents helped you to achieve your special moment?'

Now swap roles and repeat the activity!

14.5 A Positive Selfie!

Take a selfie and print it out. Place it into the picture frame below, taking care to stick it down firmly!

Next write around the edge of your picture – record all the positives you can think of about yourself – write down everything that you and others think and say!

Highlight all of your positive thinking, feeling and doing habits!

Session 15

Reflect, Evaluate & Persist!

Introduction & Aims

In this session the focus is primarily on supporting the group to reflect upon their development in terms of managing negative feelings and thoughts, including their understanding of their own strengths, skills and positive attributes. They are encouraged to further reflect upon the strategies that work for them and to set appropriate future goals and targets in this area in order to further develop and maintain the habit of effective thinking. They are also provided with the opportunity to feedback as to how useful or otherwise the contexts and delivery of the sessions was for them.

The key aims are as follows:

- For group members to have time to reflect upon what they have learnt about their thinking and how to keep a positive mindset.

- To encourage group members to articulate their best or preferred future, to visualise this, and then to describe it in detail, using the sentence starters provided.

- For group members to articulate their own personal goals and use a framework to rank these in terms of difficulty, so that they can understand the need to take and make small steps to success, rather than becoming overwhelmed by the enormity of any one task.

- Group members also have the opportunity to undertake a personal review of their learning on the course, identifying key aspects and areas for possible future development.

- Group members are finally asked to give feedback on the contents, structure and delivery of the course in order to provide useful information to help the planning of future courses.

Warm-up Activity

The warm-up activity is a circle-time game entitled 'Crossfire'. You will need three or four soft balls or beanbags to play. The first player begins with the ball and calls another player's name before throwing the ball to them. The player who receives the ball calls another player's name in turn, and throws the ball to them. The game continues in this manner – the object being that each player must remember which person they are receiving the ball from and sending it to. The ball travels by the same route to the same players each time.

You may wish to complete two or three rounds in this way before introducing a second or third ball. The new ball travels by a different route, with each player naming a new person to send the ball to. You could use different coloured balls or beanbags to make the game easier (but this is not essential). The game requires the group to avoid distraction and focus only on their part in the game (in order to avoid missing the ball and causing confusion). The balls will eventually fall and this is part of the fun of the game.

Once you have played 'Crossfire', you can introduce a second, more focused, circle-time activity. Ask the group to turn their thoughts for a moment to all the topics they have covered in this programme. Reference can be made to a visual prompt on the whiteboard/flip chart. Then re-introduce one of the balls or beanbags. As in 'Crossfire', each player names another player before throwing the ball to them. When the ball is received, the person receiving is asked to complete the following statements:

- The topic I enjoyed the most was …
- The topic I found hardest was …

Icebreaker - A Question to Thought-Storm

The group can be asked to focus upon a key question in order to prompt thinking and awareness around some of the most important issues to be covered in this session. It will be essential to encourage everyone to participate and generate their own responses, but also to ensure that everyone feels safe in doing so. The responses can be recorded on a whiteboard or flip chart, as appropriate, and you can also highlight any similarities and differences in the responses. The idea is to begin to encourage a deeper level of thinking around the key issues via the process of cooperative idea-sharing.

The key question for this session is: What have we learnt about our thinking and how to keep a positive mindset?

Case Study & Questions for Discussion

Jason wants to be a sports coach. He knows that he has a lot to learn and will need to work really hard if he is to succeed, because the competition to get onto the course he wants is really quite tough. He is not particularly brilliant at any one sport, but does know how to teach and encourage others to develop their skills. The problem is that he is finding it hard to maintain his confidence and self-belief. He had a really good report from his PE teacher last term and also some good feedback from the coach at the local pool when he was on a work experience and coaching primary age swimmers. However, he just seems to have fallen into a bit of a rut with coaching the under 11s at school and not really expanding his skills into other areas. He is also very aware that others in his year group who want to follow the same route are getting far more experience than he is and that this is going to look much better when they make their application for the course. He feels that this is not fair and that they are getting more chances, simply because the teachers like them better. He basically feels that he is losing confidence and that his chances of achieving his dream are getting slimmer.

- What kind of thoughts do you think Jason is having?

- What are the main pressures he seems to be experiencing at the moment and where do these come from?

- How might his 'negative thinking trap' be affecting him? Why is this counterproductive?

- Is he right in thinking others are getting more or better opportunities than he is? Where is the evidence for this?

- Is he right to compare himself to others and is this actually helpful to him?

- Do people have to learn how to maintain their motivation levels and self-belief levels? What might be the benefits of being able to do this?

- If you were his friend, what advice would you give him now?

- How can he break this cycle and where might he get the best help to do this?

Activities

15.1   My Best Future

For this activity, ask everyone to think about and articulate what their best or preferred future would look like. If necessary, prompt them to visualise this and then describe it in detail using the sentence starters provided on Worksheet 15.1.

15.2   My Mountain

Ask the group to write or draw all of their goals and the things they would really like to do on a piece of paper. Next, they can cut them out and arrange them on the mountain illustration on Worksheet 15.2. Ask them to place the ones that seem easiest to achieve at the bottom of the mountain, the most difficult at the top and the slightly easier ones in the middle. The group can then start with the easiest tasks and focus on these as tasks to complete first. When they've achieved these, they can then climb a little further up the mountain and try the next one. The aim is to reinforce the importance of taking smaller steps in order to reach the top of the mountain and finally achieve their goal.

15.3   My Personal Review

This is intended to be a personal review of the learning undertaken during the whole programme, using Worksheet 15.3. Explain to the group that this feedback will not be shared with any other group members, but that it will provide useful information for you and will help you to plan future sessions.

15.4   My Evaluation of the Group Sessions

Ask everyone to complete Worksheet 15.4, a final evaluation of the programme. This contributes further to the feedback process and will be especially helpful in supporting you while reviewing and amending the structure, content and delivery of the sessions.

Feedback & Reflections

Ask the group to reflect upon what they have learnt in the session, posing the following questions:

- What was useful for you in this session?

- What might have made the session more useful for you?

- What have you learnt about yourself in today's session?

- What have you learnt about others?

- How will you use your knowledge and skills to help yourself and others in the future?

The aim is to ensure that the group are able to reflect upon their knowledge and skills and also specifically to identify how and when they might transfer these into new situations in the future.

Session 15   Reflect, Evaluate & Persist!

15.1 My Best Future

What would your best or preferred future look like? Visualise this and then describe it in detail using the sentence starters below.

I will be _____

_____

I will look like _____

_____

I will feel like _____

_____

I will think _____

_____

I will act like _____

_____

I will have _____

_____

I will believe _____

_____

I will be with _____

_____

I will live _____

_____

I will _____

_____

15.2 My Mountain

Write or draw all of your goals and the things that you would like to do on a piece of paper. Cut them out and then arrange them on the mountain below.

Place the ones that seem easiest to achieve at the bottom, the most difficult at the top and the slightly easier ones in the middle.

NEXT – start with the first and easiest task – when you've achieved it, climb a little further up the mountain and try the next one. Remember – take SMALL steps to reach the TOP!

Hardest

Easiest

15.3 My Personal Review

Use this form to give your feedback about the group sessions you have attended on this programme. This feedback will not be shared with anyone else in the group but will provide useful information for your group leader to help them plan future sessions.

Rate the following statements on a scale of 1 to 10

I understand what is meant by 'effective thinking'.

1	2	3	4	5	6	7	8	9	10
disagree				neither agree or disagree					agree

I can identify my own negative automatic thoughts and test these out.

1	2	3	4	5	6	7	8	9	10
disagree				neither agree or disagree					agree

I can identify stressors in my life.

1	2	3	4	5	6	7	8	9	10
disagree				neither agree or disagree					agree

I have skills for coping with stress in my life and can use these on a daily basis.

1	2	3	4	5	6	7	8	9	10
disagree				neither agree or disagree					agree

I could support a friend who is using ineffective thinking.

1	2	3	4	5	6	7	8	9	10
disagree				neither agree or disagree					agree

I can identify my core beliefs and influences and know how to distinguish between those that are positive and negative.

1	2	3	4	5	6	7	8	9	10
disagree				neither agree or disagree					agree

I can use effective skills to solve problems and set SMART targets for myself

1	2	3	4	5	6	7	8	9	10
disagree				neither agree or disagree					agree

15.4 My Evaluation of the Group Sessions

Complete the following sentences, to give further evaluation and feedback on the sessions you have attended.

The activity I enjoyed most was _____
_____
_____

The activity I enjoyed least was _____
_____
_____

Something I have learned is _____
_____
_____

I would like to learn more about _____
_____
_____

The most useful part of the course was _____
_____
_____

The least useful part of the course was _____
_____
_____

Something I would change about the course is _____
_____
_____

Any other comments _____
_____
_____
_____

Appendices

1 Information for Parents and Carers

What is Cognitive Behavioural Therapy (CBT)?

Consent Form for the Programme

Suggestions for Parents, Carers & Teachers on Managing Anxiety

Mental Health Fact Sheet

2 References & Bibliography

CBT with Children & Young People: Useful References

Outcome Literature

Assessment References

Appendix 1

Information for Parents & Carers

What is Cognitive Behavioural Therapy (CBT)?

CBT focuses on the links between thoughts, feelings and behaviour, especially the way that unhelpful thoughts lead to and maintain distressing feelings and behaviours that can be a problem.

The therapeutic process aims to help the person to identify, understand and change both unhelpful thoughts and behaviours in order to feel better and be able to function more effectively in everyday life.

CBT is usually short term, structured and focuses on dealing with current problems and difficulties, rather than trying to uncover causes in the distant past. The therapist and the young person talk and undertake activities together to help with this process.

The Use of CBT Tools and Strategies in this Xourse

This programme does not provide individuals with therapy, but focuses on introducing and practising a range of key tools and strategies, which will aid positive and effective thinking and the maintenance of overall well-being. Sessions involve goal-setting, problem-solving and trying out new skills and ways of thinking. In between sessions there will be some assignments for the week, for example keeping a 'thought diary', practising skills learned in the session and trying out new ways of dealing with real life situations.

Agreement to participate in the sessions

We always ask for signed consent for young people to participate in this kind of programme, and I would be grateful if you could complete this consent form.

If you have any queries or questions then do please contact us at the school on

_____ .

I agree to let my child participate in the Effective Thinking Programme and understand that these sessions will aim to support their skills in effective thinking and their overall well-being.

Signed _____ (parent/carer)

I agree to participate in the programme.

Signed _____ (pupil)

Appendix 1

Suggestions for Parents, Carers & Teachers on Managing Anxiety

Learning to manage anxiety is an important life skill. The following are some ways in which parents/carers can assist children and young people to handle anxiety:

Appendix 1

- Support them to challenge underlying beliefs and thoughts – negative and irrational beliefs and thoughts such as, 'If I don't look perfect, no one will like me,' or 'I can't cope with difficult or scary situations,' are significant factors in generating anxiety. Model and communicate effective ways to question and challenge anxiety-provoking thoughts and beliefs.

- Support them to accept uncertainty – uncertainty is one thing that people worry about a lot because of the potential for negative outcomes. As it is impossible to completely eliminate uncertainty, you can assist children and young people to be more accepting of uncertainty and ambiguity.

- Be a role model – if you can manage your own anxiety, young people will see that it can be managed and incorporate your strategies into their own behaviours. Teaching parents to manage their own anxiety has been shown to be helpful in reducing their children's anxiety.

- Be patient – sometimes the behaviours of anxious children and teens may seem unreasonable to others. It is important to remember that an anxious young person who cries or avoids situations is, in fact, responding instinctively to a perceived threat. Changing avoidant behaviours takes time and persistence.

- Balance reassurance with new ideas – when a child comes to you with something they are worried about, listen and understand what is happening. Explore with them what they could do to manage their fears.

■ Show children and young people some simple relaxation techniques – deep breathing, progressive muscle relaxation and meditation can be helpful as a way of learning how to better manage physical anxiety symptoms. Generally these techniques are only effective if practised consistently over several weeks.

■ Encourage plenty of physical exercise and appropriate sleep – when people are well-rested and relaxed, they will be in a better mental state to handle fears or worries.

■ Moderate the consumption of caffeine and high sugar products – caffeine products (including cola and energy drinks) increase levels of anxiety as they cause energy levels to spike and then crash. This leaves a person feeling drained and less able to deal with negative thoughts.

■ Make time for things that the child enjoys and finds relaxing – these could be simple things such as playing or listening to music, reading books or going for walks.

■ Help them to face the things or situations they fear – learning to face their fears and reduce avoidance of feared objects and situations is one of the most challenging parts of overcoming anxiety. Facing fears usually works best if it is undertaken gradually, a step at a time.

■ Encourage help-seeking when needed – make sure that children and young people know there are people who can help if they find that they cannot handle a problem on their own. Knowing that they can call on others for support if needed will make them feel less anxious about what might happen in the future.

■ Ask for a referral from your GP – you may have to do this if you suspect a child is suffering from an anxiety disorder. By assisting children and young people to learn effective ways to handle anxiety, you can ensure that they are able to deal with it later in life.

Appendix 1

Mental Health Fact Sheet

What is Mental Illness?

There is no precise definition as to what constitutes mental illness, but it is considered to be a condition that may affect the way we feel and think, resulting in an inability to cope with every day social interactions and routines. Although often considered to be rare, as many as one in four adults may suffer from a form of mental health problems every year and these often begin in childhood. The mental health problems suffered by adolescents in our schools include: depression, anxiety, eating disorders, phobias, personality disorders and obsessive compulsive disorders.

What Causes Mental Illness?

Mental illness is a misleading term, because many mental health disorders may have a physical or biological component. For example, those who have a close family member who suffers from depression are more prone to it themselves. Some medications and hormonal changes may also lead to forms of mental illness. Environmental and social factors may include poverty, stress and trauma. Often it is a combination of factors that leads to mental illness.

What are the Signs of Mental Illness in Young People?

In adolescents warning signs may include the following:

- Frequent outbursts of anger
- Changes in eating habits, perhaps leading to considerable weight gain or weight loss
- A prolonged negative mood
- Frequently complaining of physical problems, for example headache, stomach-ache
- Challenges to authority such as theft, truancy and vandalism
- Alcohol or drug abuse
- Sleeplessness

Appendix 1

How Can I Improve my Own Mental Health?

- Avoid substances that are depressants, such as alcohol and tobacco or other drugs.

- Allow yourself plenty of time for a form of relaxation you enjoy. Physical exercise is particularly useful in combating depression.

- Eat a healthy balanced diet.

- Talk to others about how you are feeling. Hiding your feelings will not make the problem go away and things may build up.

- Set yourself goals and prioritise your challenges.<BL*>

How Can I Get Further Help?

If you continue to feel depressed or anxious, you may need to seek expert help. To do this you should visit your GP who should be able to help you access the support you need. This might include a referral for counselling, medication such as anti-depressants or a referral to community mental health team specialist such as a psychiatrist. It is advisable to seek help early to reduce negative outcomes as a result of your illness.

Appendix 1

Appendix 2
References & Bibliography

CBT with Children & Young People: Useful References

Barrett, P. & Turner, C. (2001) 'Prevention of anxiety symptoms in primary school children: Preliminary results from a universal school-based trial', *British Journal of Clinical Psychology*, 40, pp399–410.

Ben-Shahar T. (2007) *Happier: Learn the Secrets to Daily Joy and Lasting Fulfilment* New York: McGraw-Hill.

Bousted Mary, ATL Survey Association of Teachers and Lecturers (2013), 'Disruptive behaviour in schools and colleges rises alongside increase in children with behavioural and mental health problems', http://www.atl.org.uk/Images/disruptive-behaviour-on-rise.pdf

Butler G. & Hope T. (1995) *Manage Your Mind: the Mental Fitness Guide.* Oxford: Oxford University Press.

DfES (Department for Education and Skills) (2004) *Every Child Matters: Change for Children in Schools,* London: DfES.

Department of Health (2008) 'Improving Access to Psychological Therapies (IAPT) Commissioning Toolkit', Norwich: DOH.

Department of Health (2004) 'DOH National Healthy Schools Programme', Norwich: DOH.

Department of Health (2001) 'Treatment choice in psychological therapies and counselling', London: HMSO.

Doherr L., Reynolds S., Wetherly J. & Evans E.H. (2005) 'Young children's ability to engage in cognitive therapy tasks: Associations with age and educational experience', *Behavioural and Cognitive Psychotherapy*, 33, pp201–15.

Dummett N. (2006) 'Processes for Systemic Cognitive-Behavioural Therapy with Children, Young People and Families', *Behavioural and Cognitive Psychotherapy*, 34, pp179–89.

Dunsmuir S. & Lyadurai S. (2007) 'Cognitive Behavioural Therapy: Effectiveness, expertise and ethics', *Debate*, 122, pp15–20.

Farrell P., Woods K., Lewis S., Rooney, S., Squires G. & O'Connor, M. (2006) DFE research report RR792 'A review of the functions and contributions of Educational Psychologists in England and Wales in the light of Every Child Matters: Change for children', London: DfES.

Fonagy P. & Target M. (1998) 'An interpersonal view of the infant', in A. Hurry (ed.) *Psychoanalysis and Developmental Therapy*. Monograph series of the psychoanalysis unit of U.C.L. and the Anna Freud Centre. London: Karnac Books.

Ford T. (2014) 'Schools: a public health frontier or the Wild West', University of Exeter, The Behavioural and Brain Sciences Unit, London. Lecture 26 June 2014.

Frank E. & Rush A.J. (1994) 'The therapeutic relationship with adolescents', in J.C.R. Wilkes et al. (eds), *Cognitive Therapy for Depressed Adolescents*. New York: Guilford Press.

Friedberg R.G. & McClure J.M. (2002) *The Clinical Practice of Cognitive Therapy with Children and Adolescents: the Nuts and Bolts*. New York: Guilford Press.

Gourley, P. (1999) *Teaching Self-control in the Classroom: a Cognitive Behavioural Approach*. London: Sage.

Graham P. (2006) *Cognitive Behaviour Therapy for Children and Families*. Cambridge: Cambridge University Press.

Graham P. (2005) 'Cognitive behaviour therapies for children: Passing fashion or here to stay?' (Jack Tizard lecture), *Child and Adolescent Mental Health*, 10 (2), pp57–62.

Greig A. (2001) 'A framework for the delivery of Cognitive Behaviour Therapy in the educational psychology context', *Educational & Child Psychology*, 24 (1) pp19–35.

Greig A. & MacKay T. (2005) 'Asperger's syndrome and cognitive behaviour therapy: new applications for educational psychologists', *Educational and Child psychology* 22, pp4-15.

Green, H., McGinnity, A., Meltzer, H., Ford, T. & Goodman, R. (2005) *Mental Health of Children and Young People in Great Britain*, 2004, Office for National Statistics on behalf of the Department of Health and the Scottish Executive. London: Palgrave MacMillan.

Harrington, R. (2000) 'Cognitive behavioural therapies for children and adolescents', in M.G. Gelder, J.J. Lopez-Ibor & N.C. Andreasen (eds), *New Oxford Textbook of Psychiatry*. New York: Oxford University Press.

Hobday A. & Ollier K. (1998) *Creative Therapy: Activities with Children and Adolescents*. Leicester: BPS Books.

Holmes J. (2002) 'All you need is cognitive behaviour therapy?', *British Medical Journal*, 324, pp288-290.

Kendall P. (2000) *Child and Adolescent Therapy: Cognitive Behavioural Procedures*, 2nd edn. New York: Guilford Press.

Kendall P. & Lochman J. (1994) 'Cognitive Behavioural Therapies', in M. Rutter et al. (eds) *Child and Adolescent Psychiatry: Modern Approaches*. Oxford: Blackwell Scientific.

Kennerley H. (2000) *Overcoming Childhood Trauma*. London: Constable & Robinson.

Kennerley H. (1996) 'Cognitive therapy of dissociative symptoms', *British Journal of Clinical Psychology*, 35, pp325–40.

London School of Economics (2007) MHEEN II Policy briefing January 2007 LSE PSSRU Project supported by the European Commission, Directorate General for health and consumer protection.

Mackay T. (2002) 'Review of the provision of educational psychology services in Scotland (The Currie report)', Edinburgh: Scottish Executive.

McAdam E. (1987) 'Cognitive behaviour therapy: Working with the troubled adolescent', in J. Coleman (ed.), *Working with Troubled Adolescents*. London: Academic Press Inc. (London) Ltd.

Appendix 2

McNamara, E. (1998) *The Theory and Practice of Eliciting Pupil Motivation: Motivational Interviewing – A Form Teacher's Manual and Guide for Students, Parents, Psychologists, Health Visitors and Counsellors.* Ainsdale, Merseyside: Positive Behaviour Management.

McNamara, E. (1992) 'Motivational Interviewing: the gateway to pupil self-management', *Pastoral Care*, September, pp22–8.

Miller W.R. & Rollnick S. (1991) *Motivational Interviewing: Preparing People to Change Addictive Behaviour*, New York: Guildford Press.

OECD (2014) 'Teaching and learning international survey of secondary school teachers', http://www.keepeek.com/Digital-Asset-Management/oecd/education/talis-2013-results_9789264196261-en#page1

Prochaska J.O. & Diclemente C.C. (1982) 'Transtheoretical Theory: Toward a more integrative model of change', *Psychotherapy*, 20, pp161-173.

Ronen T. (1997) *Cognitive Developmental Therapy with Children.* Chichester: Wiley.

Salkovskis P.M. (1996) 'The cognitive approach to anxiety: Threat beliefs, safety seeking behaviours, and the special case of health anxiety and obsessions', in P.M. Salkovskis (ed.), *Frontiers of Cognitive Therapy.* New York: Guilford Press.

Seligman M. (2011) *Flourish: A new understanding of happiness and well-being and how to achieve them.* London: Nicholas Brealey Publishing.

Squires G. (2001) 'Using cognitive behavioural psychology with groups of pupils to improve self-control of behaviour', *Educational Psychology in Practice*, 17 (4), pp317–35.

Stallard P. (2005) *A Clinician's Guide to Think Good – Feel Good. Using CBT with Children and Young People.* Chichester: Wiley.

Stallard P. (2002) *Think Good – Feel Good: A Cognitive Behaviour Therapy Workbook for Children and Young People.* Chichester: Wiley.

Weare K. (2000) 'Work with young people is leading the way in the new paradigm for mental health – commentary', *International Journal of Health Promotion*, 4(4) pp55-58.

Westbrook D., Kennerley H. & Kirk J. (2007) *An Introduction to Cognitive Behaviour Therapy: Skills and Applications.* London: Sage.

Outcome Literature

Carr A. (ed.) (2000) *What Works with Children and Adolescents: A Critical Review of Psychological Interventions with Children, Adolescents and their Families.* London: Routledge.

Fonagy P., Target M., Cottrell D., Philips J. & Kurtz, Z. (2002) *What Works for Whom? A Critical Review of Treatments for Children and Adolescents.* London: Guilford Press.

Ollendick T.H. & King N.J. (2000), 'Empirically Supported Treatments for Children and Adolescents: Advances toward evidence-based practice', in P. Kendall (ed.), *Child and Adolescent Therapy: Cognitive Behavioural Procedures*, 2nd edn. New York: Guilford Press.

Wolpert M., Fuggle P., Cottrell D., Fonagy P., Philips J., Pilling S., Stein S. & Target M. (2006) *Drawing on the Evidence: Advice for Mental Health Professionals Working with Children and Adolescents*, 2nd edn. London: CAMHS Publications. www.camhs.org.uk/documentdownload.aspx?doc=DotEBooklet2006.pdf

Assessment References

Anxiety Disorders Interview Schedule for DSM-IV: Child Version
Silverman W.K. & Albano A.M. (1996) *Manual for the Anxiety Disorders Interview Schedule for DSM-IV: Child Version*. USA: Graywind Publications.

Revised Children's Manifest Anxiety Scale (RCMAS)
Reynolds C.R. & Richmond B.O. (1985) *Revised Children's Manifest Anxiety Scale*. Los Angeles: Western Psychological Service.

State–Trait Anxiety Inventory for Children (STAIC)
Spielberger C.D, Gorsuch R.L., Lushene R., Vagg P.R. & Jacobs G.A. (1983), *Manual for the State–Trait Anxiety Inventory for Children*. California: Consulting Psychology Press.

Spence Children's Anxiety Scale (SCAS)
Spence S.H. (1998) 'A measure of anxiety symptoms among children', *Behaviour Research and Therapy*, 36, pp545–66.

Social Phobia and Anxiety Inventory for Children (SPAIC)
Beidel D.C., Turner S.M. & Morris T.L. (1995) 'A new inventory to assess childhood social anxiety and phobia: The Social Phobia and Anxiety Inventory for children', *Psychological Assessment*, 7, pp73–9.

Social Anxiety Scale for Children (SCAS)
La Greca A.M., Kraslow Dandes S., Wick P., Shaw K. & Stone W.L. (1983) 'Development of the social anxiety scale for children: Reliability and concurrent validity', *Journal of Clinical Child Psychology*, 17, pp84–91.

Fear Survey Schedule for Children – revised (FSSC-R)
Ollendick T.H. (1983) 'Reliability and validity of the revised fear survey schedule for children (FSSCR)', *Behaviour Research and Therapy*, 21, pp685–92.

Multidimensional Anxiety Scale for Children (MASC)
March J.S., Parker J.D.A., Sullivan K., Stallings P. & Conners K. (1997) 'The Multidimensional Anxiety Scale for Children (MASC): Factor Structure, Reliability and Validity', *Journal of the American Academy of Child and Adolescent Psychiatry*, 36, pp554–65.

Screen for the Child Anxiety Related Emotional Disorders (SCARED)
Birmaher B., Khetarpal S., Brent D., Cully M., Balach L., Kaufman J. & McKenzie Neer S. (1997) 'The Screen for Child Anxiety Related Emotional Disorders (SCARED): Scale Construction and Psychometric Characteristics', *Journal of the American Academy of Child and Adolescent Psychiatry*, 36, pp545–53.

Child Behavior Checklist (CBCL)
Achenbach T.M. & Edelbrock C.S. (1991) *Manual for the Child Behavior Checklist and Profile*. Burlington: University of Vermont.

Appendix 2

Children's Depression Inventory (CDI)

Kovacs M. (1981) 'Ratings scales assess depression in school-aged children', *Acta-Paedopsychiatrica*, 46, pp305–15.

Beck Youth Inventory

Beck J.S., Beck A.T. & Jolly J. (2001) *Beck Youth Inventory*. Toronto: Psychological Corporation.

Psychology in Education Portfolio

Frederickson N. & Cameron R.J. (eds) *The Psychology in Education Portfolio*. Windsor: NFER-Nelson.

Portfolio of Measures of Children's Mental Health & Psychological Wellbeing

Frederickson N. & Dunsmuir S. (eds) *Measures of Children's Mental Health & Psychological Wellbeing*. Windsor: GL Assessment.

See booklets (each containing six measures) on:

- Belonging
- Distress
- Enjoyment
- Healthy Living
- Social Behaviour
- Resilience
- Responsiveness